GROWN APART

How to WIN BACK Your Spouse

Written by
Matt and Pam Loehr

Grown Apart: How to WIN BACK Your Spouse

Written by Matt & Pam Loehr
DareToBeDifferent.com
RefreshYourMarriage.org

Edited by Kelly Lipin, Clear Message Editing & Review

Copyright © 2020 Dare to be Different, Inc.
ISBN 978-1-7345975-0-9
First Edition

Printed in the USA

This book is dedicated to every person or couple that value the sanctity of marriage and who will do what it takes to not only have a good marriage, but a God-honoring marriage.

Contents

walk into the pain

navigate your family through the valley

communicate with love and respect

lift your own spirit

be a servant

in sickness and in health

affirm and encourage

guard your heart

endure through the storm

go on a quest

slow and steady

put on the armor of God

define victory, then seize it

let's start this journey together

A Word from Matt and Pam

Are you frustrated with your spouse? Are they being difficult, refusing to change, and unwilling to get help? Maybe they even believe that you're the problem? Has busy life caused one or both of you to take your eyes off the relationship, and you seem to have grown apart? Does one of you want out of the marriage? Are you separated, with thoughts of divorce looming over you? If you are looking to find out what it will take to save your marriage, this book is for you.

Perhaps you've already pursued books, seminars, workshops, and/or church activities in search of answers. But none of your efforts have been successful and you feel stuck.

Regardless of the marital strife you are encountering, this guide will equip you to fight for your marriage and win your spouse over using biblical principles based on God's promises.

First Peter 3:1 challenges wives who live with unbelieving husbands to "win them over" without words. In 1 Peter 3:7, husbands are told to "Be considerate with your wives, lest your prayers be hindered." Ephesians 5:33 encourages husbands to be loving and wives to be respectful. These concepts will be used throughout this guide, enabling you to achieve your goal.

You are about to begin what could be a life-changing journey. In the next fifty-two weeks, you will learn what it means to fight for your marriage God's way and to be an authentic follower of Jesus Christ through what may be the most difficult time of your life.

Our Mission

Our goal is for you to strengthen or save your marriage. This fifty-two-week study guide is a starting place to strip away the clutter and help you discover (or rediscover) your identity in Christ, despite the difficult and daunting circumstances you face.

This book will put you on a path where God can work in and through you and eventually reach your spouse because of your actions, your commitment, and your prayers. Through you, your spouse may come to a saving relationship with Jesus Christ, pursuing Him like never before, eager to seek divine help for your marriage.

This process will allow you to identify some of your own issues and walk away with a solid, lifelong plan that will enable your heart to be healed and transformed.

Get the Most Out of This Experience

Each week we will give you specific instructions: *what to say, what to do, what to read,* and *what to pray* (and in some situations, *what not to do*). By following this twelve-month plan, you will see God's love and redeeming power in your marriage like never before. Commit to each week's challenge and let God do the rest.

Finding someone to hold you accountable to the process is key to your success. Meeting monthly with this person to encourage, challenge and hold you accountable to each week's requirements will not only benefit you, but also your marriage. It's recommended that they also have a copy of this book so they know what is required of you each week.

Remember the objective of this book is to win back your spouse. That means loving the unconventional way in the present moment... even when it's hard.

Need Help?

Our online marriage mentoring program is often times that extra necessary step for complete marriage restoration. As you work through this book, when you sense the time is right, ask your spouse if they will join you in getting help. If they say yes, visit refreshyourmarriage.org to get connected with a certified mentor couple who can help you. Mentoring through our online video course can be life changing, and can make your marriage everything it was meant to be.

Let's get started!

Matt and Pam Loehr

Founders of Dare to be Different

walk into the pain

Week 1

Start with Repentance

Someone once asked me (Matt), "How do I save my marriage?" I responded with, "Repent of your sins and forgive your spouse for theirs."

This seems like an easy solution. And it is, in theory. However, it can be one of the most difficult tasks to carry out. As you begin your first week on this journey, get down on your knees and ask the Lord to forgive you for your part of the broken or strained relationship. Be specific with God as you pour out your heart to Him.

I'm guessing that you are wounded, tired, and lonely. I am sorry for the heavy burden you're under. But I'd like to help you save your family and stop the Enemy from destroying your marriage. If you choose to be strong and fully engage in this battle, you can win it!

The first thing you must commit to is facing your pain rather than running away. Many people run away from their pain, which leads to broken relationships and allowing wounds to define their lives and spill over into their children. If you face your pain like a warrior running into battle, you can be victorious for your family. Running into your pain may seem a bit confusing. Let me break it down into three thoughts. First, choose to remain engaged verbally with the person who wounded you. Second, remain committed to serve the person who wounded you. Third, remain soft-hearted towards the person who wounded you so you can be led by the Holy Spirit. God will shape your response to the wound so you don't act out in a way that would grieve the Holy Spirit and sabotage your mission. Applying this approach enables you to live life as a warrior for Christ rather than a wounded soul who is weary, exhausted, and rendered paralyzed. You may be thinking, "Does that make me a door mat?" No, by no means. There are ways to confront, defend and at times exit a relationship to protect your wellbeing. However, we will address that later. It's too soon to expect your spouse to be 'won over'. Let's wait one month before we try to get them to take action steps towards you or God.

For you, repentance is the first step.

> If my people who are called by my name would humble themselves and pray and seek my face and turn from their own wicked ways, I would hear from heaven, forgive their sin and heal their land.
>
> 2 Chronicles 7:14

Countless times in Scripture God connects our repentance to His healing power. There is no other bridge you can cross to find healing in your marriage, your heart, or your home. Repentance is the only way to unleash God's power in your life.

If you want to win over your spouse, begin by acknowledging the areas in your life that grieve the Lord. Then humble yourself and confess your sins to your spouse. Don't expect them to melt into your arms and forget about everything. It may take months or even years for them to accept your apologies.

My mother and father survived years of betrayal and hopeless situations. But they found God's healing power and spent the second half of their marriage thriving. Why? They believed their marriage was worth fighting for. They humbled themselves, prayed, sought God, and turned from their selfish ways. And they received God's healing.

what to say

- Tell your spouse you are sorry for your part in the strained relationship, that you are committed to changing and working on yourself.

- Wife, tell your husband, "I'm sorry for coming across as disrespectful. I am going to work on being more respectful toward you."

- Husband, tell your wife, "I'm sorry for coming across as unloving. I am going to work on being a more loving husband."

- Be as specific as you can about what you are sorry for and how you are going to change. Your mission is to create a safe place to share concerns and frustrations. There is no doubt your spouse has issues that need to be addressed, but first you have to convince them that your marriage is worth fighting for.

what to do

- Do two things this week for your spouse that are loving and respectful.

- If you can't deliver your apology in person, write a letter of repentance. Then give it to your spouse or place it in an area you know they will find it.

- Accept your spouse's blame, even if their allegations are inaccurate. Their perceptions are reality to them, just like yours are to you. Telling them you're sorry will diffuse their attack.

- Share your concerns with unbiased believers who can help hold you accountable.

Caution: Don't use texts, email, or social media to argue, defend, or try to resolve relational issues. The best method of conflict resolution is face-to-face.

Separation

Being separated leads to divorce far more often than it leads to reconciliation. While separated, every day that goes by, your family would get used to living separate lives, which creates an ever-higher wall between you and your spouse. It also opens the door to temptations to interact with the opposite sex.

If you are already separated, don't move back in together if it would create an unsafe environment or if one of you is battling a chronic issue, such as an addiction or serial cheating. Don't move back in together if you (or your children) are physically at risk of harm. But with the exception of such extreme circumstances, make every effort to stay together while getting help.

what not to do

- Don't retaliate.
- Don't defend yourself.
- Don't be unloving or disrespectful.
- Don't share your frustrations with family members or friends of the opposite sex.

what to read

- Proverbs 28:13
- Acts 3:19
- James 5:16
- 2 Peter 3:9
- 1 John 1:9

what to pray

Lord Jesus, I repent of all my sins against You and against my spouse. Please forgive me. I ask You to do a healing work in me that spills over into my family. Give me a supernatural ability to love, respect, and serve my spouse. Give me a supernatural ability to endure my own pain and wounds so I can lead my family to a better place.

I lift my spouse up to You, Lord. I ask You to begin the healing process for both of us. I pray that You would soften my spouse's heart so they can hear You and feel my love as I start on this quest. I pray for our children, Lord, that they would not be wounded too deeply by what we are going through. Protect them. Give me the words to say and the things to do that would redeem this marriage.

In Your holy name I pray. Amen.

notes

_____

_____

_____

_____

_____

_____

_____

_____

_____

_____

_____

_____

_____

_____

_____

_____

_____

_____

_____

Week 2

Understand Forgiveness

Forgiveness is one of the most powerful things you will ever do in your life. It leads to freedom, happiness, joy, and healthy living. I have witnessed the destruction of unforgiveness and seen the devastation it leaves behind.

I got to know Sandy and John very well as we mentored them. Things really seemed to be progressing in the right direction. After watching God perform miracles in their lives, John fell back into an alcohol addiction two years later. We attempted to help them again, but this time Sandy was done. John had broken his promise once again, which left Sandy feeling hopeless. Unforgiveness overtook her. John became remorseful and finally checked himself into rehab, but it was too late. Sandy had given up and divorced him.

You may want to punish your spouse for their sin, but resist the temptation. You may believe with all your heart that you are right and they are clearly wrong, but withhold your judgment and offer mercy instead. Don't allow your mind to obsess over their sin. Instead remember all the times God has forgiven you and extended mercy to you. It removes the sting just a little. Give them time to be transformed by God. It may take years.

God tells us to "forgive and be forgiven" (Matthew 6:14).

God tells us to "forgive seventy times seven" (Matthew 18:21-22 NASB).

God tells us to "love your enemy and become children of the Most High" (Luke 6:35).

If forgiveness isn't evident in your life, it's possible you haven't truly forgiven. Here are some visible signs that you've forgiven your spouse:

- You give them affection (hold their hand, give back rubs, hugs, etc.).
- You initiate romance and intimacy.
- You initiate conversation.
- You serve them (cook dinner, perform house duties, etc.).
- Your heart is tender toward them.
- You pray for them.
- You show them respect, even though they may not deserve it.
- You show them love, even if they do not earn it.

You can say you forgive your spouse but still hold unforgiveness in your heart. God knows. Some people think forgiveness should not be given unless the other person repents first. That does not line up with Jesus's teaching. He didn't say, "Forgive seventy times seven if they repent that often."

Forgiveness doesn't mean you let your spouse continue to sin. You can forgive someone, give them affection, and still verbalize your disappointment with their actions. Forgiveness doesn't mean you endorse their sin. But it enables you to proceed with the relationship without holding them and yourself hostage.

Forgiveness is a gift you give yourself. It keeps your heart soft and open to God.

Don't let unforgiveness become a toxic chemical that flows from you onto others. Let God avenge you. Live in the land of freedom.

You will never win your spouse over without forgiving, over and over and over.

With the power of the Holy Spirit within you, you can forgive your spouse. And when you do, you will feel a huge weight lifted.

what to say

- "I want you to know that I am truly sorry if I have hurt you or offended you in any way.
- "I choose to love you even though I don't feel like it sometimes."
- "I am praying for God to help me manage my anger."

Caution: Be careful not to let anger and despair drive you to decisions you may regret.

If your spouse is physically abusing you or has a chronic behavior that causes an unsafe environment, you can still forgive them. But remove yourself from the environment to protect yourself and your children. You can love your spouse from a distance until they prove themselves trustworthy and rehabilitated from their harmful behavior.

what to do

- Choose to forgive your spouse in your heart. Then show that forgiveness by doing something kind for them: a long hug, a foot massage, giving flowers or a card, cooking a nice meal.
- Tell your spouse you have forgiven them.
- Tell your children you are choosing to forgive your spouse and ask them to do the same.
- Send your spouse a loving and respectful text message or email.
- If you fall back into unforgiveness, repent and start over.

what <u>not</u> to do

- Don't talk negatively about your spouse behind their back.
- Don't allow your heart to grow cold by shutting down and withholding affection.
- Don't allow your children to choose the path of unforgiveness and turn against your spouse. (Remember, your spouse is their father/mother and always will be).
- Don't create an alliance against your spouse by choosing a team of supporters who will only side with you.

what to read

- Matthew 6:12-15; 18:32-33
- Mark 11:25
- Luke 17:3-4
- 2 Corinthians 2:6-11
- Ephesians 4:31-32
- Colossians 3:12-14

what to pray

Dear merciful Lord, I thank You for the power of forgiveness. Help me to be quick to forgive and also quick to ask for forgiveness. When I forgive in words, allow Your Holy Spirit to fill my heart with peace. I pray that the peace that comes only from Jesus will rule in my heart, keeping out doubt and questions. Help me find the compassion that comes with true forgiveness.

Help me to walk in righteousness, peace, and joy, demonstrating Your love. Help my spouse to forgive me for my shortcomings and help them to have the mind of Christ. Take any ungodly thoughts captive and make them obedient to You, Lord. Your Word says to "put on love, which binds everything together in perfect harmony" (Colossians 3:14 ESV). Help us both to demonstrate unconditional love toward one another. In Jesus's name, amen.

notes

_____

_____

_____

_____

_____

_____

_____

_____

_____

_____

_____

_____

_____

_____

_____

_____

_____

_____

_____

_____

_____

_____

_____

_____

_____

_____

_____

_____

_____

_____

_____

_____

Week 3

Plan Your Journey

We live in a world of immediate gratification and entitlement. Most people hate the word wait. Many uproot their lives and move on if someone or something doesn't serve them as well as they'd like. That was never God's design, especially regarding the covenant of marriage.

God's timing is often much slower than ours. King David was promised the crown, but he endured years of punishment from Saul before God intervened and fulfilled that promise. Moses led the Israelites through the wilderness for forty years before they entered into the Promised Land. Abraham wasn't able to have the son God promised until he was one hundred years old.

This fifty-two-week guide is a one-year plan to help you win your spouse over to Jesus and to you. One year gives God the time to work in your situation and soften your spouse's heart so they will turn toward you, your family, and God. If you faithfully follow this guide and wait on the Lord to show Himself, you too will receive God's blessings.

what to say

- "I will work on giving you the love and respect God wants me to give you."
- "I am committed to our marriage and am sorry for how I have hurt you."
- "I am going on a quest to find ways to improve myself, to serve you, and to strengthen our relationship."

what to do

- Mark your calendar one year from now as a reminder of your goal. It's not the end of your journey, but it is the end of the first phase.
- Continue to give your spouse the message that you are in this for the long haul through loving greeting cards (handmade cards or handwritten notes are best), text messages, and one-on-one conversations.
- Anticipate rejection, but make a commitment to endure.

what not to do

- Don't get on an emotional roller coaster by following your feelings of despair, loneliness, anger, frustrations or lust.
- Don't give up.
- Husband, don't show your wife unloving behavior because you feel her disrespect.
- Wife, don't show your husband disrespect because of his unloving behavior.
- Don't make yourself available to the opposite sex while you are vulnerable.
- Don't forget about the impact your decisions have on your children.
- Don't spend a lot of time with people who are encouraging you to "get out, divorce, move on."

what to read

- Psalm 37:7; 40:1
- Romans 5:3-5; 12:10-12
- Philippians 4:11-13
- Hebrews 6:12, 10:35-36
- James 1:2-4
- James 5:7-8
- 2 Peter 1:5-9

what to pray

Dear Lord, I ask You to give my family and me the strength to cope during this crisis we are facing. Help us to love each other and become united through these trials. Equip me with a supernatural patience, and help me to trust in your timing rather than forcing my own schedule. Give me hope that someday we will be restored to trust, peace, and faith. In Jesus's name, amen.

notes

_____
_____
_____
_____
_____
_____
_____
_____
_____
_____
_____
_____
_____
_____
_____
_____
_____

Week 4

Expect Turbulence

Your spouse may not respond positively to you for weeks, for months, or even at all. And things may get worse before they get better.

Satan is not happy with your goal because it represents the very essence of Jesus's final prayer, that we all become one so the world will know who sent Him (John 17). What you are doing has the potential to bring your spouse, your children, and all those watching your family closer to God. The Enemy hates that. He will not idly sit by and let you lead people to Jesus.

Turbulence may show up in a variety of ways; a poor response to an unmet expectation, withdrawn behavior, turning to someone or something outside of the marriage, or spiritual complacency.

If you anticipate turbulence, you can prepare for it emotionally, spiritually, and physically. Seek a godly friend that can encourage you, pray for you, and be there for you when you are having a tough day. Hopefully that friend is already going through this process with you to hold you accountable.

Your spouse may not change at all. They might reject your quest despite the conviction of the Holy Spirit in their lives. But keep in mind, they are ultimately rejecting God, not you. Let God work. Be aware of your own shortcomings and when they surface, deny their demands. You will want to defend and avenge yourself, however, the Bible tells us God is to be our avenger (Romans 12:19). Often, your immediate feelings are driven by your flesh and not the Lord. Delay your response and then discover God's whisper. Follow His leading.

You can take the path the world takes by giving up on your marriage because it's hard. Or you can take the narrow path, led by the Holy Spirit, and receive a far greater reward.

This journey is going to be hard. But God is with you. He will go before you. And He will send people to come alongside you. Trust in Him with all your heart and don't lean on your own understanding. Then He will make your path straight (Proverbs 3:5-6).

what to say

- "We're going to have setbacks and that's okay. It's improvement that I am praying for."
- "Things may be difficult right now, but I'm trusting God and know we can endure."
- "I played a role in our situation, and I want to change any behavior that has pushed you away. Please be patient with me as I seek God and allow Him to make me into all that He wants me to be."
- "It's okay if you don't trust me. My goal is to earn your trust, and I will work hard to make that happen."

what to do

- Speak in a way that conveys respect, gentleness, and humility. When turbulence occurs, control your thoughts, words, and actions so you will draw your spouse close to you, not push them away.

- Husband, show love and kindness to your wife when things get turbulent. She is wounded, and she doesn't trust you. Your consistent behavior will inspire her to turn her heart back to you.

- Wife, show respect to your husband when things get turbulent. Your consistent respect will have a huge impact on him. He will begin to feel hopeful and trust that your respect is authentic which will increase his desire to turn his heart back to you.

what not to do

- Don't fall back into your old patterns when you're wounded.
- Don't respond in the flesh by yelling, cursing, or threatening divorce.
- Don't expect your quest to change your spouse overnight.

what to read

- 2 Chronicles 15:7
- Psalm 27:14; 37:23-24; 42:5, 138:8
- John 16:33
- 1 Corinthians 15:58
- Galatians 6:9
- 2 Thessalonians 3:13
- Hebrews 4:15-16
- James 4:7-8

what to pray

Heavenly Father, You are intimately aware of the struggle I am experiencing—the pain and the despair. Even though I feel wounded, I know my emotions don't have to control my actions. Father, may Your sweet words saturate my mind and direct my thoughts. I pray the same for my spouse. Help them release the

21

hurt and love as Jesus loves. You know the desire of my heart for my marriage and family to be restored. I ask for Your healing touch. I praise You for the work You are doing in my life, teaching and perfecting my faith. In Jesus's name, amen.

notes

navigate your family
through the valley

Week 5

Include Your Children

No matter how young or old your kids are, make them a part of your quest. Couples often try to isolate their children from the turbulence in their marriage, but they are typically far more aware of the situation than their parents think.

If you don't communicate your plan to your kids, they will imagine the worst of conditions and outcomes. By including them you can show them the power of God at work in your hearts, and teach them how to face turmoil in their future relationships. You can also show them how to honor both parents and not "pick sides," regardless who seems right or wrong.

It's imperative to not pit your children against your spouse, purposely or unintentionally. This becomes a wrecking ball and is extremely hurtful. It can damage the relationship between your children and your spouse, and can undermine any chance of reconciliation with your spouse down the road.

Children don't know how to manage their emotions in a healthy way. They can't process data the same way as adults. Keep things vague, yet encourage them to share their feelings at any time.

Show your kids that you love, respect, forgive, and honor your spouse. They will see the value of your choices and will follow your lead. Because of your example, they will learn how to forgive and grant mercy. These are huge life lessons that can be a struggle even for adults.

what to say (to your children)

- "I love you very much, and I want you to know that what is going on between Mom and Dad is not your fault. We are working on our marriage."
- "I want to pray for our family. Will you join me?"
- "Would you be open to getting counseling as a family, so we can all get to a healthy place?"
- "I'm sorry if I've hurt you in any way, and I ask for your forgiveness."
- "I forgive your father/mother for what they have done, just as God has forgiven me of my sins. I ask you to do the same."

what to do

- Plan a family meeting to discuss your situation. Prior to the meeting, prepare in private with your spouse. Come to an agreement on what will be discussed and who will say what. This is not a time to air all the ways your spouse has failed you, but rather an opportunity to share the circumstances with your children and give them a chance to express their feelings.
- Stay connected with your children by having weekly conversations about how they are feeling.
- If your children are acting out or having a hard time adjusting, seek Christian counseling.
- Pray for and with your children. Encourage them to pray aloud with you.
- Teach your children biblical principles, including forgiveness, repentance, kindness, patience, and faith in Jesus Christ.

what to read

- Deuteronomy 2:7
- Deuteronomy 12:28
- Psalm 103:17
- Proverbs 11:21; 22:6
- Isaiah 44:3; 54:13
- Ephesians 6:4
- Colossians 3:21

what to pray

Lord, I pray Your emotional, physical, and spiritual protection over my children. Keep evil far from them, and help them to trust You as their refuge and strength. Guard their minds from harmful instruction and grant them discernment to recognize truth. Make them strong and courageous in our situation. Help them to find peace in Your presence. Let them know that the only safe place is in Jesus. Amen.

notes

_____

_____

_____

_____

_____

_____

_____

_____

_____

_____

_____

_____

_____

Week 6

Affirm Your Spouse to Your Children

My (Matt) father never spoke negatively about my mother, though he had reasons to do so. He even confronted us kids when we said anything negative about her.

One day, when I was in my thirties and my father in his seventies, I went fishing with him. I brought up some recent conflict I had with my mother, hoping for some sympathy. His response startled me: "Son, that's my wife you're talking about. She isn't perfect, and sometimes she's wrong. But I never want you to disrespect her like that again."

It's okay for children to vent with respect, but if they vocalize their anger and disrespect your spouse, confront them in love by asking them to be careful with their words. Remind them that their mother or father isn't perfect (none of us are), and they need to show mercy and forgiveness. Ephesians 6:2-3 tells us to honor our mother and father and receive the promise of a long life with God's blessing. There isn't an asterisk next to that verse giving children permission to dishonor to their parents, because they feel like complaining.

Proverbs 18:21 tells us words have the power to build up or destroy others. As often as possible, affirm your spouse verbally in front of the kids and avoid saying things that tear them down.

At times it will seem impossible to find positive words to say about your spouse. But continuing to shame them will only sabotage your marriage.

what to say (to your children)

- "I appreciate your mom (or dad) because ..."
- "The things I cherish most about your mom (or dad) are ..."
- "The greatest thing I've ever seen your mom (or dad) do was ..."
- "I love the way your mother (or father) ..."
- "Don't say anything bad about your mom (or dad). I won't allow it."
- "We will get through this as a family, but I need your commitment to never pick sides between me and your mom (or dad). Can you do that?"

what to do

- Praise your spouse in front of the children.
- Ask your children to write three things about your spouse they appreciate most.
- Play a game at your next family meal. "Let's go around the table and share one reason we're grateful for _____ (your spouse's name)."

what not to do

- Don't slander your spouse to your children (or anyone else).
- Don't leverage your children against your spouse. Keep from sharing details of your circumstances that would make yourself look better or more fun than your spouse.
- Don't allow your children to pick sides.

what to read

- Psalm 50:23
- Proverbs 13:3; 18:7-8, 21
- Matthew 12:36
- Luke 6:45
- Ephesians 4:29-32
- 2 Timothy 4:2
- James 1:26; 3:6, 10-11

what to pray

Heavenly Father, enable me to speak kindly of my spouse to our children. Help me to make a positive difference in their hearts. When I find it difficult to find encouraging words, I pray You will reveal to me all the positive attributes my spouse contributes to our marriage and family. In Jesus's name, amen.

notes

_____

_____

_____

_____

_____

_____

_____

_____

_____

_____

_____

_____

_____

_____

_____

Week 7

Pray Over Your Children

God wants us to bring our burdens to Him. In Matthew 11:28 Jesus says, "Come to me, all you who are weary".

Praying with and for your children is one of the most impactful activities you can perform for their personal and spiritual development. It gives them a strong sense of security. It shows you care. It lets them see that you put your faith in God front and center. It places their needs at the foot of the cross, trusting God to respond. It teaches them how to do the same for their children.

If you've never prayed over your children, it may be awkward at first. The more you do it, the easier it will be, and it will develop into a habit.

Pray for anything that comes to mind. Pray for their safety, their life, their hearts, their future. Pray for your spouse and your family too.

Saying grace before meals can be a nice way to start praying out loud in front of your family. Take turns to get everyone involved. It's possible that over time your spouse will be deeply impacted by your effort to bring prayer into the home. After all, the one common passion you and your spouse will always share is the well-being of your children.

If you aren't a Christian, read Romans 10. It says we all fall short of God's righteousness, but if we repent of our sins, confess that Jesus Christ is Lord, and believe in Him, we will be saved. If you've never taken this step, ask Jesus to be your Savior now. He will enter your heart and secure your salvation for all eternity. Ask Him to show Himself to you. He will. And when He does, share it with someone.

what to say (to your children)

- "I am praying for you. Is there anything specific you'd like me to pray for?"
- "I want to start praying over our meals before we eat. Let's start doing that today."
- "Can I pray for you before you go to bed?"

what to do

- Pray over meals with your children.
- Start praying with your children at bedtime.
- Make praying a family ritual.

what to read

- Matthew 18:18-20
- Romans 10
- Philippians 4:6-7
- Hebrews 4:16

what to pray

Lord, I want to be a godly example to my children. I desire for them to develop an eternal perspective and purpose. I pray that You will bring godly friends into their lives and give them the discernment to select their friends wisely. I pray they will come to understand the extent of Your love for them, which surpasses all the head knowledge they could acquire. I pray they will be filled up with You from morning to night. In Jesus's name, amen.

notes

Week 8

Worship Together

If you're a member of a church family, take advantage of this network of people who share the same beliefs and spiritual goals. Seek their support and encouragement through this challenging time. If you don't have a home church, I urge you to find one where you feel comfortable.

Taking your children to church every week provides them with security and consistency. On the way home from church, ask them what they heard and what they think about it. Encourage them to ask questions. Such discussions can lead to powerful conversations that will strengthen the bond between you.

Being active in faith-based church programs will offer your family a wealth of discussion topics, which will aid in facilitating meaningful conversations.

I encourage you to require your children to attend church with you until they are at least sixteen. At that point, you can let them know that you want them to continue pursuing the Lord, but that it's time for them to make a decision for faith on their own. Help them transition from being under your leadership to being their own individuals, and pray that they choose to continue pursuing God.

If your spouse isn't interested in attending church, it's even more important for you to take your children there with you so they can learn the fundamentals of who God is and what His Word teaches. They need to know where to turn when life throws them a curve ball.

what to say (to your children)

- "I would like to get more involved in church. Other than going to services every week, can you think of ways we can get involved and serve?"
- "What do you like about our church? What don't you like?"

what to do

- Commit to worshipping together as a family.
- Encourage your kids to get involved in the youth or children's ministry.
- Use sermons as conversation starters with your children.
- Take responsibility for the spiritual development of your kids.

what to read

- Colossians 1:9-14
- 1 Timothy 4:16
- Titus 2:7-8

what to pray

Heavenly Father, I pray that You would instill in my children a desire and passion to go to church, where they can freely worship Your holy name. I pray that they will set their minds on things above and be rooted and grounded in Your love. Help them to see life's challenges through Your eyes and be eager and unafraid to share with others the good news of Jesus wherever they go. In the precious and holy name of Jesus, amen.

notes

communicate with love and respect

Week 9

Words Can Bring Healing

Words have the power to help and heal.

One way to bring healing to your marriage may be to change how you communicate with your spouse. Do you yell? Call names? Nag? Accuse? If so, commit to breaking the patterns of the past and learn how to communicate in a way that draws your spouse closer to you.

The first step is to recognize your responsibility. Don't blame your spouse for your poor communication habits.

Before speaking, take a few moments to contemplate what you will say, considering the impact your words will have on your spouse.

Always speak the truth. Avoid exaggerating. Be consistent in what you are saying. Share your feelings, but remember your feelings aren't right or wrong, they're just feelings. Share them with love and respect. Don't use your words to manipulate. And most important, don't use words to insult or belittle your spouse.

Kind words are beacons of inspiration, enthusiasm, and encouragement. Not only do your words matter, but the tone you use matters as well. Speak in a way that solidifies peace and compassion.

My friend and ministry partner, Emerson Eggerichs PhD is author of New York Times best seller, *Love & Respect*. This marriage book reveals why spouses react negatively to each other and how they can deal with such conflict quickly, easily and biblically. It is changing the way couples talk to, think about, and treat each other.

what to say

- "I know we don't have a perfect relationship, but I love you. Will you join me in getting counseling or mentoring?" or "Will you go to church with me?" or "Will you move back in with me?" or "Will you give us another chance?" Pick the right one that fits your situation.
- "I need you, our family needs you, and I will always fight for you."
- "How can I make things better for you?"
- "Today is all about you. What would you like to do?"

what to do

- Greet your spouse at the door when they get home from work. Stop whatever you're doing and kiss them.
- Ask their advice on something—and then follow it (without challenging them).
- Brag about your spouse to your friends when your spouse can hear you.

what to read

- *Love & Respect* by Dr. Emerson Eggerichs (go to loveandrespect.com for more information)
- Proverbs 12:18; 15:4; 16:24; 17:27-28
- Ephesians 4:29

what to pray

Father, help me to always bring out the best in others, particularly my spouse. Help me to bless them with kind words, give the gift of encouragement, and speak words of life. Thank You for filling my heart with affirmation so I can affirm those around me, especially my spouse, today and every day. In Jesus's name, amen.

notes

_____
_____
_____
_____
_____
_____
_____
_____
_____
_____
_____
_____
_____
_____
_____
_____
_____
_____
_____
_____
_____
_____
_____
_____

Week 10

Words Can Bring Destruction

Be cautious when talking to your children, your friends, and your family about your spouse. Anything you share could get back to them and erode their trust in you. Harsh words can give your spouse ammunition against you.

Be careful what you say to your spouse as well. Contemptuous words like accusations, name calling, criticism, degrading or being overly negative will demotivate your spouse to do what you want … or what God wants. Even if you feel you have good reason for being full of contempt, disrespect will breed unloving behavior, which in turn leads to more disrespect. The more times you blow up in anger, the more convinced your spouse will be that leaving you is the right thing to do. But what would happen if you controlled your sharp tongue and found a positive way to communicate your frustrations? If you were loving when you expressed your concerns and respectful when you responded to him?

When strife occurs in your marriage, you may feel like your spouse is the enemy. Or perhaps you feel like they treat you as the enemy. Romans 12:20 challenges us to feed our enemies when they're hungry and give them water when they're thirsty, to overcome evil with good. You can do this by having a controlled response to your spouse's anger and using words that are carefully delivered in a way that shows love, joy, peace, patience, kindness, goodness, faithfulness, gentleness and self-control (Galatians 5:22-23).

A man can win his wife over if he consistently uses loving words. Likewise, a woman can win her husband over with consistent words of respect.

Laurie L. Dove reveals the power of positive and negative comments in her article titled "The Criticism Ratio:"

> For every criticism, we should provide at least five positive comments. This ratio is as true for interpersonal relationships, such as marriage, as it is for professional relationships. Research that analyzed married couples' success rates finds the largest indicator of whether a couple will stay wed is not religion, shared values or children. It's the ratio of criticism to compliments. Couples who make five positive comments for every negative comment are more likely to stick it out. And the couples who eventually divorce? The ratio was nearly equal: three positive comments for every four negative comments.
>
> So, is the goal to refrain from criticism? Absolutely not. It's an essential ingredient in achieving success in relationships, whether at home or at work. Criticism gets our attention. It shakes us out of complacency. It can even fuel our success.
>
> But the behavior-changing elements of criticism are not enough to sustain. We need positive encouragement, too. It motivates us to continue on, work harder and try more. Criticism, it turns out, is just one side of the coin. We need a carrot and a stick. Or, more accurately, five carrots for every stick.[1]

You are not your spouse's supervisor, parent, or corrections officer. For every critical comment that comes out of your mouth, compensate with at least five positive comments.

Encourage your children to do the same.

When you feel the need to confront your spouse about something negative, first answer the following questions about the issue:

- Is this the right time to bring it up?
- Is it necessary that I share this?
- Have I determined the most kind way to say it?
- Have I recently shared too many negative concerns?
- Do I have the right attitude and motive?

what to say

If it's the right time and necessary, use the following statements when sharing your concerns.

- "It really hurts me when you ..."
- "It would mean a lot to me if you would stop/start ..."
- "I need _____ from you."
- "I really appreciate _____ about you; however, when you _____, it makes me feel _____ ."

what to do

- Pray before you enter into conflict. Ask God to help you be loving and respectful.
- If you feel angry, take time to reflect on your poor behavior before you engage in conversation.
- When you blow it, repent. Tell your spouse you are trying to improve.
- In a daily journal, document all the positive and negative

comments you share with your spouse. Analyze whether you've given at least five positive comments for every negative one.

- Before speaking to your spouse, write out your words so you can deliver them carefully and thoughtfully.

what to read

- Proverbs 10:19; 13:3; 15:1-2; 18:21; 25:18
- Matthew 15:11
- Colossians 4:6

what to pray

Father, I ask forgiveness for all the negative and harmful words I have spoken about and to my spouse today. Transform my thoughts and let me understand Your unfailing love. Change my heart and my habits so I can speak favor upon my spouse and create a positive atmosphere in my home. In Jesus's name, amen.

notes

_____

_____

_____

_____

_____

_____

_____

_____

_____

_____

_____

_____

_____

_____

_____

Week 11

What, When, How, and How Often

Poor communication is often related to poor timing or poor delivery.

Jim and Lisa met at a fitness center. They had an immediate physical attraction to each other and started dating. Before long, they discovered they saw everything in life through different lenses. At first, they bantered on minuscule issues. As their relationship progressed, the bantering turned to arguing, hurt feelings, and anger. They began to wonder if they had a future together.

They knew that if they did get married, they needed to improve their communication style. Eventually Jim and Lisa realized that neither of them was right or wrong; they were simply different. Having learned how to handle conflict unselfishly, they wed and had a happy marriage.

Take a good look at your communication style. Have you found a healthy way to embrace the differences between you and your spouse? Or are you stuck in the rut of constantly verbalizing your opposing views?

If you've developed negative patterns, work on changing the way you communicate.

When?

If your spouse shares an opinion and you have a different perspective, consider whether there is any purpose or benefit from expressing your opinion. Not every hill is worth dying on.

If you decide it's important to share your opposing view, assess your spouse's attitude. Do they have an open mind and an open spirit? If not, wait for a better time to speak.

Don't contradict your spouse in front of others, especially the children. Hold your tongue until you're alone.

Before you open your mouth to speak, make sure you've really heard what your spouse said. Proverbs 18:13 tells us, "He who speaks before he listens is a fool." Listening never made a person foolish, but speaking often does.

How?

Before you share your opposing opinion, use affirming words. For example, "I see your point." Pause here; perhaps even share positive thoughts about your spouse's point. "But here's another thought." Or, "That's a great idea. Have you considered _____?" After expressing your suggestion, follow up with more affirmation.

How Often?

No one wants to constantly hear opposing views. So only share yours when necessary or when asked. Cut your opposition in half and see what happens to your relationships and your attitude.

what to say

- "I'm working on the way I communicate with you and others. I want to be a better listener and speak in a way that makes you feel heard and validated."
- "I'm sorry I've hurt you with my words. I want to be less critical and more sensitive."

- "I appreciate the way you _____." (Share one new thing each week)

what to do

- Count how often you verbalize your opposing views to people each day. Try to cut that number in half.
- Write down affirming and encouraging comments and place them in your spouse's path.

what to read

- Psalm 39:1; 141:3
- Proverbs 21:23
- 1 Thessalonians 5:11
- 1 Peter 3:9-10
- James 1:19-20; 3:5-8

what to pray

Father, thank You for looking beyond my faults and for loving me unconditionally. Forgive me when I fail to love others in the same way. Give me eyes to see the needs of the difficult people in my life and show me how to meet those needs in a way that pleases You. Give me opportunities to show my spouse the love of Christ through my words and actions to draw them closer to You. In Jesus's name, amen.

notes

_____
_____
_____
_____
_____
_____

Week 12

Stay Engaged

Stonewalling is a term that describes a person being uncooperative, obstructive, or evasive; refusing to comply or cooperate with someone else. Stonewalling can be passive or aggressive. You can use it to protect yourself from being wounded or to punish your partner. Either way, it's unhealthy for a marriage because it stalls communication. Stonewalling doesn't actually protect you from getting hurt; it only causes you more pain through a hardened heart.

If your spouse is stonewalling, stay engaged. Try using small talk. Ask them open-ended questions about things that won't trigger a fight such as, "What can I make you for dinner?" That forces them to engage and lets them know you're trying. When two people shut down, there's no hope for a healthy relationship.

Tom's wife told him she was finished with their marriage. She avoided any conversation with him regardless of his kind and gentle attempts. He couldn't penetrate her shield. This poured over into their children as they were feeling the same impact. For several months, Tom remained engaged, trying to connect with her. He would often say, "You look nice" or "Have a great day" as she walked out the door for work. He relied on the Lord and put his trust in God's ability to reach his wife. Eventually, she felt remorse for giving him the cold shoulder. Not only did she begin to open up to him, but they ended up getting the help they needed through marriage mentoring. To this day their marriage is thriving.

Staying engaged with your partner will give God a chance to reach them through you. Even if you don't see any change in your spouse, your children will learn how to handle conflict by watching you.

You will need to exercise patience in this process. Remember, it took your spouse years to get in the valley of stonewalling. That won't change overnight.

If your spouse goes cold, comfort them with a warm blanket of affection and draw them back into your arms by showing love and respect.

what to say

- "I know you're hurting and I am here for you."
- "It's been a while since we've been on a date. Can I plan a date night for us?"
- "I love you and am committed to you, even though times are difficult."
- "I'm sorry for my part in our issues. I'm working on myself and ask for your patience with me."

what to do

- Plan a date night that involves activities your spouse enjoys doing, even if they're not things you enjoy.
- Purchase Discovery Cards from daretobedifferent.com and use them on a date night to connect and communicate with your spouse. These great, insightful questions can help renew your relationship in a fun and non-threatening way.
- Go for a walk with your spouse.
- Write a letter to your spouse, sharing all the things you appreciate about them.

- Give affection (hug, hold hands, make eye contact).
- Stay engaged.
- Visit refreshyourmarriage.org to get connected with a certified mentor couple who can help you.

what to read

- Psalm 34:18; 147:3
- Jeremiah 29:11
- Luke 6:27-36
- Romans 8:18-28
- 2 Corinthians 1:3-8

what to pray

Lord, thank You for the people You have placed in my life who speak holy truth, love, and words of wisdom. Give me a heart of discernment to know when You are using someone to speak instruction into my heart and my circumstances, and give me the strength and courage to follow through with that advice, even when it's hard. Fill me with peace in knowing that even if I take a wrong turn, Your purpose will prevail. In Jesus's name, amen.

notes

_____
_____
_____
_____
_____
_____
_____
_____
_____
_____

Week 13

Stand on the Bible

God's Word is alive! The more you immerse yourself in the Word, the more He will reveal to you. To know God better, you must spend time listening to Him. The Bible is His message to you. If you want Him to hear you when you pray, you should listen to what He has to say. He will be your compass. His Word is the perfect road map for your life.

God can speak directly to our hearts. But the Enemy will try to deceive you, making you think that his words are from the Lord. If you know His written Word, you can judge whether or not the guidance you're hearing is from God. Prayerfully reading the Scriptures is the only defense against being misled.

One of the main reasons God brings or allows trials in our lives is to cause us to seek Him more fervently, recognizing in a fresh, new way how dependent we are upon Him. Reading the Bible every day will lift your spirit, educate your mind, and create a shield of protection from the Enemy. Spending quiet time with God allows you to connect with the true healer, the source of your strength, the one who can transform and sustain you.

When you're hurting, Psalms is a great book to read. The Gospel of

John will teach you about Jesus and his gift of salvation. Proverbs will help you attain and apply wisdom to daily living as well as provide moral instruction. Whatever you read in the Bible, allow God to speak to you through His living words.

Pray that God will help you understand His Word and apply its principles to your life. James 4:8 tells us that if we come near to God, He will come near to us. Seek Him and you will find Him (Jeremiah 29:13). No matter how difficult your trials, seek the Lord's wisdom and trust Him to work for His glory and your good.

what to say

- "I am committed to reading the Bible regularly so I can follow God's leading and become a better spouse." (This will help your spouse understand that you are working on yourself).
- "I have a lot of room to grow spiritually, and I want to learn and understand more about God's Word. Will you help me?"
- "Would you be open to joining a small group in our church so we can learn more about the Bible together?"

what to do

- Schedule a daily time to read the Bible.
- Journal your thoughts as you read. Write down any ideas or comments you may have as you study the Bible.

what to read

- The Gospel of John

what to pray

Lord, Your Word speaks promises of healing and restoration. Thank You for the miracles You still perform today. Today I claim those promises over my marriage. I believe in the power of faith and prayer, and I ask You to begin Your mighty work in me and my spouse. Please surround us with supernatural peace and strength, and give us the faith to believe that all things are possible with You. Protect us from Satan's lies and discouragement, and allow a miraculous healing to occur in our marriage. In Jesus's name, amen.

notes

_____

_____

_____

_____

_____

_____

_____

_____

_____

_____

_____

_____

_____

_____

_____

_____

_____

_____

_____

_____

_____

_____

_____

_____

_____

Week 14

Pray Fervently

Prayer is probably the most under-utilized tool in the Christian arsenal. Prayer is not some quaint activity employed by pastors to make worship services more interesting. And it certainly shouldn't be something we do only when everything else fails.

How would you describe your prayer life? Do you only pray over meals and occasionally during church? Or are you praying in a way that brings down fire from heaven? (See 1 Kings 18:24, 36-38).

Although I (Matt) don't consider myself a prayer warrior, my wife Pam is. Every morning she spends time in God's Word with a notebook and a list of people and situations to lift up in prayer. I often wonder if Pam's prayers are the main reason for God's blessings in my life.

When I get to heaven, I wouldn't be surprised if God told me, "Matt, your wife sent angels by the thousands into battle on your behalf. She articulated her requests and I heard her cry, commanding legions of angels to carry out her wishes. You, along with thousands of other people, were the recipient of her mighty work in prayer."

Let me share with you a few reasons I think prayer is so important in our daily lives.

Prayer puts life in perspective. Like an artist has to stand back from time to time and view his handiwork from a distance, you and I need to step away from the noise and confusion of our lives and look at ourselves from God's perspective. Prayer gives us that opportunity.

Prayer aligns us with God's will. We tend to put our own self-interests ahead of God's interests. But in prayer, we put our lives under God's control. That's what Jesus did on that dark night in the garden, when he laid out all His anxieties and fears before His Father. He didn't want to go into Jerusalem and confront His adversaries. But he prayed, "Not my will, O God, but yours be done" (Luke 22:42). That prayer didn't take away Jesus's ordeal. But it aligned His will with the Father's and it made it possible for Jesus to proceed with His assigned task. Are you willing to trust God to lead you in the right direction?

Prayer releases us from anxiety. "Do not be anxious about anything, but in every situation, by prayer and petition, with thanksgiving, present your requests to God. And the peace of God, which transcends all understanding, will guard your hearts and your minds in Christ Jesus" (Philippians 4:6-7). Prayer opens the flood gates to the resources and power of the Holy Spirit. By removing the agony of worry, it gives us energy to handle the difficult situations of life. When prayer is part of our daily routine, we open ourselves up to the inspiration of God's Spirit. Prayer provides new insights, focus, and motivation so we can take on hard tasks and cope with stress in our lives.

Let me share an example of how God moves through prayer.

Doug, an alcoholic, was separated from his wife, Jenny, and was engulfed in anxiety and despair. Pam and I met with the couple a few times to try to help their marriage. Pam encouraged Jenny to pray some specific prayers. One of those prayers was for Doug to do something inspired by God, to help her see that he was taking responsibility for his actions and that he was committed to making real changes regarding his alcohol issues.

While on a business trip in another country, Doug wrote a letter to his wife that was clearly inspired by God. Here are some excerpts from that letter:

Hi, Jenny.

Well, I'm three hours into a fifteen-hour flight. I have enjoyed the smell of wine and booze without having a drop. I wanted to send you an email to say thank you for praying for me and for your ongoing support. To hear you say no one is cheering and praying for me more than you, warms my heart and brings tears of joy to my eyes. The last five months haven't been easy for either of us. However, our struggles may be what I needed to finally realize I had to grow up and be a better husband and father.

I want you to know the old Doug was gone the moment I got baptized in Arizona. Although I can't guarantee I'll never get upset again, I can assure you the new Doug is here to stay, and I will do my very best to honor God, you, and the kids.

It has been amazing to see how God has been working and guiding us through all of this. Your strength, love, kindness, and support are an inspiration and an amazing example to me and our children.

I really believe God is working through our mentors to help us restore our marriage and family. The conversations with them are becoming less difficult and more about how God is teaching me to support and love you.

Be assured, the commitments I've made are not taken lightly. I have every intention to follow through with them, even if takes me a while to get comfortable with them. My desire and intent are to provide you with unconditional love, kindness, patience, and joy. I need your continued support, love, and coaching to get me through this transformation.

After fifteen hours on a plane I'm now in Delhi, getting ready to depart for Pune, India. Normally I would be enjoying a few Kingfisher beers, but not this time. Instead I'm enjoying sharing with you my thoughts and heartfelt intentions.

I've been thinking about our meeting with the kids. I plan to share some of this email, talk about what I've done wrong over the years (with you and them), share my love, apologize for the way I've treated you and them, and ask for forgiveness. This will not be easy. However, it's a critical step to rebuild my relationship with the kids and show my respect and love for you. I plan to pray every day this week and ask God to help me prepare my message to you and the kids.

I know you're unsure if the "new Doug" will last. And you're probably asking yourself, "How can I be sure that this time will be different?" Below are the reasons why I believe it will be.

1. Time away from you and the children has been very difficult. It has given me a lot of opportunity for self-reflection and soul-searching.

2. Since I was baptized I feel different. I have a stronger calling now to grow in my faith and my relationship with God.

3. I'm committed to continue to meet with our mentors.

4. I have honored your request to stop drinking ... one day at a time.

5. I don't want to lose you or the kids. Jenny, you're too good of a person, wife, mother, and friend to let you go!

6. This time I really want to change and am committed like I've never felt before.

7. Most important, I do not want to lose you and will fight for you and our marriage!

I hope this helps you see that this time is different and will result in a different outcome. Jenny, we have too many blessings and gifts to not give this our very best and make it work. I truly believe our best days are ahead of us! Well, it's 11:00 p.m. in India. Just finished working out and didn't have a beer, wine, or mixed drink. Tomorrow will be two weeks. One day at a time.

Love you forever!

Doug

This letter became the turning point in Doug and Jenny's marriage. It gave Jenny the confidence that God truly was working on her husband. They fully reconciled, Doug moved back in, and he found freedom from his bondage. All that came from one wife's commitment to prayer.

Pray in your own way. Write down your thoughts, pray out loud, or say speak to God in your heart. Articulate your needs, your beliefs, your wants, and your wishes. Pray that God will change you, that He will change your spouse, that He will bring your spouse to their knees if brokenness is what it takes for them to believe, trust, and follow His ways. Pray for God to give you patience and endurance. Pray for your children to not be negatively hurt by your situation. Pray for a miracle. Pray that God would move in a specific way and change the course of your situation. God isn't overwhelmed with details. He is the author of them.

Be patient. God may not respond as quickly or exactly as you wish, but He will respond. Document the specifics of how God answers your prayers and review the list from time to time.

what to say

- "I am praying for you."
- "Is there anything you'd like me to pray about for you?"
- "I'm putting my hope and trust in God and His ability to answer my prayers."

what to do

- Wife, purchase the book *The Power of a Praying Wife* by Stormie O'Martian. Husband, purchase *The Power of a Praying Husband*. Read one chapter a day.

- Journal your prayers. Occasionally look back and see how God answered them.

- In addition to asking God to help your marriage, praise Him, glorify Him, and thank Him, even in the midst of your pain. Read in Psalms how David shouted out to God during his times of despair. He asked for help and gave God glory at the same time. He worshipped God in his prayers. You can too.

- Write out a prayer for your spouse and leave it on the counter for them to find before they leave for work (or when they get home).

what to read

- 1 Chronicles 4:9-10
- Psalm 3; 51
- Proverbs 3:5-6
- Matthew 6:9-13
- Mark 11:24

- Colossians 4:2
- 1 John 5:14

what to pray

Dear Father God, thank You for Your unfailing love for me, Your blessings, and Your goodness. I am thankful that I can come to You for anything. Thank You for Your faithfulness to guide me and see me through times of uncertainty, for lifting me up and setting me on high. Thank You for Scripture that comforts and reminds me of Your promises, plans, and provision. Thank You for taking away my fears and worries and for reminding me that my help comes from You. In Christ's name, amen.

notes

_____
_____
_____
_____
_____
_____
_____
_____
_____
_____
_____
_____
_____
_____
_____
_____
_____
_____
_____

Week 15

Get Plugged In

It's important to get plugged into a small group, Bible study, or support group. Christianity is meant to be relational—first on a vertical axis between ourselves and God, and second on a horizontal axis between ourselves and those around us. Small-group Bible studies move us from being spectators in a weekly church service to active participants in a like-minded community dedicated to spiritual growth.

As we encounter God's Word together, we have opportunities to share our different perspectives, and insights are broadened. More information is retained when there is active involvement, so biblical literacy is enhanced. Application and accountability bring understanding that moves God's Word from the mind to the heart. Transformation is encouraged and lives are changed.

We all need friends to help weather the storms of life. Relationships require an investment of time and a level of vulnerability and trust. Hebrews 10:24-25 says we should "consider how we may spur one another on toward love and good deeds, not giving up meeting together, as some are in the habit of doing, but encouraging one another."

In a group Bible study you can celebrate life's victories, get prayer support, be encouraged in tough times, and keep yourself accountable in your personal growth. It can be a safe place to work out the challenges you face. Thriving marriages are usually surrounded by loving people.

Galatians 6:2 tells us to "carry each other's burdens and in this way, we fulfill the law of Christ." Imagine a group of people literally lifting your arms when you're tired, hugging you when you're lonely, giving you water when you're thirsty and food when you're hungry.

Perhaps you don't feel comfortable exposing your burdens to godly people. Maybe you feel guilty or embarrassed. Or you're a very private person. Take a chance, get out of the boat, and see what God can do when you open up to another believer. It's probable they will love you, cry with you, encourage you and even challenge you.

When we wrap our lives around each other as Christians, the "law of Christ is being fulfilled" as seen in Galatians 6:2. If all you do is attend church on Sunday and go home without any interaction with fellow believers, you're missing out on the most important part of God's church.

what to say

- "I would like to join a small group. Would you be interested in joining me? (If your spouse says no, don't get angry. And don't let that deter you from pursuing a small group on your own).

what to do

- Call your church and ask about joining a small group. If your church does not have small groups, get involved in a community Bible study.

what to read

- Numbers 11:17
- Proverbs 27
- Matthew 11:28
- Galatians 6:2

what to pray

Father God, my heart is filled with chaos and confusion. I feel as if I'm drowning in my circumstances, and I am overcome with fear and frustration. I need hope. I need the strength and peace that only You can give. I know that You are able to do far more than I could ever ask or imagine. I'm hopeful that You are restoring and redeeming every place of difficulty, every battle, for Your greater glory. In Jesus's name I pray, amen.

notes

_____

_____

_____

_____

_____

_____

_____

_____

_____

_____

_____

_____

_____

_____

_____

_____

_____

Week 16

Be Grateful in the Midst of Uncertainty

In the midst of your turmoil and uncertainty, you may wonder what there is to be grateful for. In the midst of your suffering, there is still beauty, goodness, and kindness all around you. You need only open your eyes to see the tiny ray of light. Hope is close by, waiting for you to receive it.

I encourage you to be grateful for what you have. Look beyond what is lacking in your life and open your heart to the abundance that is before you. Gratitude is the key to accessing the present. But to enter we must leave all negative thoughts at the door.

Two psychologists, Dr. Robert A. Emmons of the University of California, Davis, and Dr. Michael E. McCullough of the University of Miami, have done much of the research on gratitude. In one study, they asked all participants to write a few sentences each week, focusing on particular topics. The findings were written about in Healthbeat, by Harvard Health Publishing:

> One group wrote about things they were grateful for that had occurred during the week. A second group wrote about daily irritations or things that had displeased them, and the third wrote about

events that had affected them (with no emphasis on them being positive or negative). After 10 weeks, those who wrote about gratitude were more optimistic and felt better about their lives. Surprisingly, they also exercised more and had fewer visits to physicians than those who focused on sources of aggravation.[2]

Though storms may be troubling you right now, what joy can you see in your life? What amazing things has God done for you?

what to say

- "I am so grateful for ..."
- "Moving forward I am going to choose an attitude of gratitude. I'm sorry for the times that I haven't shown my appreciation for you and all you do. I really do appreciate you."

what to do

- Begin and end your day with a prayer of gratitude and a clear intention to be more grateful.
- Write a thank-you note to your spouse.
- Keep a gratitude journal. List at least ten things you're grateful for each day. Focus on people (your spouse particularly), situations, or events.
- Take your spouse out to lunch or dinner as a gesture of gratitude.
- Buy someone a cup of coffee.
- While on a walk or a drive, look for the beauty around you.

what to read

- Psalm 126:3

- Philippians 4:6-7
- Colossians 3:15-17
- 1 Thessalonians 5:16-18

what to pray

Father, I am sorry for the way I complain about my circumstances. Please forgive me for my bad attitude when things don't go my way. I want to see Your hand in every part of every day, good or bad. Help me learn how to face every storm with confidence, knowing that You are in control even though I may not be able to hear Your voice or see Your hand at work. In Jesus's name, amen.

notes

_____

_____

_____

_____

_____

_____

_____

_____

_____

_____

_____

_____

_____

_____

_____

_____

_____

_____

_____

_____

be a servant

Week 17

Don't Follow Your Feelings

"Follow your heart" sounds simple, beautiful, and liberating. But our hearts were not designed to be followed. God intended them to be led.

Feelings are temporary and not always true. If you allow your emotions to guide you, you'll be like a yo-yo, with your happiness tied to circumstances you can't control.

Take control of your feelings. Don't allow others to control them. No one can *make* you angry. No one can *make* you love them. No one can *make* you worry. And no one can *make* you happy.

In Hebrews 3:10 God tells us our hearts are always going astray. Be mindful of what our hearts tell you. When you let Him drive your decisions and reactions, peace will blossom. You'll become more grounded, the negative will turn positive, and joy will fill your heart.

Compare your emotions to what the Word of God says. If there's a discrepancy, your heart is deceiving you. Let me give you an example.

Jane was at a crossroad in her life. Based on her feelings, she was convinced God wanted her to leave her husband. After working with a mentor couple for a few weeks, she evaluated the "voice" that told her to divorce and discovered it wasn't God's but the Enemy's. Satan was feeding her lies. Instead of following her feelings, she studied the Bible and asked God to lead her. Jane found out the Bible didn't give her provision to divorce her husband just because he was moody and had a drinking problem. She discovered that God hates divorce (Malachi 2:16 NASB), and then she read where Jesus said unless it be for sexual unfaithfulness, we ought not divorce (Matthew 19:8-10). As a side note, we believe there are other provisions for divorce that aren't so 'spelled out' in scripture such as abandonment, physical abuse, severe emotional abuse and similar extremes. Jane turned back to her husband and found levels of joy and happiness.

The real point here is to contrast your inner thoughts with the Word of God, then you can discern their origin. The flesh always leans toward selfishness. Satan wants you to take steps that will destroy your marriage, your family, your Christian friends, and ultimately your faith in God.

When you give the Holy Spirit control of your thoughts and actions, you will be amazed at the things you can do—even serving someone who doesn't deserve it. When you are hurt, you offer kindness. When you are cursed, you offer forgiving words. When you are treated in an unloving way, you respond with respect. When you are disrespected, you offer love.

Luke 6:27-36 tells us to bless those who curse us. The next time your spouse wounds you, respond by serving them. Offer a back rub. Take them for a walk and hold their hand. Cook dinner, then do the dishes and clean up. This is the opposite of what your feelings will tell you to do. But serving the person who is hurting you can be a key step to winning them over. And blessings will follow.

Respond in ways that bring honor to God. Choose to exemplify the fruits of the Spirit: love, joy, peace, patience, kindness, goodness, faithfulness, gentleness, and self-control (Galatians 5:22-23). Instead of following your feelings, follow God!

what to say

- "I want to be able to serve you more. What can I do that's meaningful to you?"
- "I'm sorry I haven't been serving you the way I should. Please forgive me. I want to do a better job."

what to do

- Cook a meal and do the dishes.
- Give a back rub.
- Clean the house.
- Go for a walk, holding your spouse's hand.
- Give your spouse a day off by watching your children so they can do something they want to do.
- If it seems like the right time, seek a third party for help. Contact your church or feel free to contact us at daretobedifferent.com.

what not to do

- Don't digress if your spouse doesn't respond well.
- Don't just do something nice once and be done. You're on a quest. Work to make it a habit.
- Don't expect your spouse to be grateful. Serve them without expecting anything in return.

what to read

- Proverbs 12:15
- Jeremiah 17:9
- Luke 6:27-36
- Ephesians 4:18
- 1 Peter 4:10-11

what to pray

Lord, I'm weary. My energy is depleted and my motivation is lagging. I need Your strength and Your fresh touch to carry and sustain me. I know my feelings can't be trusted, so when doubt and despair overtake my thoughts, keep a condemning spirit far from my heart and even further from my lips. Your Word says *the joy of the Lord is my strength.* I need Your joy to replace all the parts of my mind and heart that can't be trusted. I ask this in Jesus's name, amen.

notes

_____

_____

_____

_____

_____

_____

_____

_____

_____

_____

_____

_____

_____

_____

_____

_____

_____

_____

_____

_____

_____

_____

Week 18

Serving Isn't Enabling

You've probably heard that serving people who are toxic enables them to continue with their unhealthy behavior. Psychologists argue that we must set and maintain proper boundaries to protect ourselves against such people.

Withdrawing from people who are living in sin seems a perfectly valid consequence. Serving them feels ... well, wrong.

Throughout the Bible, God often tells people to do things that counter human logic. "Hey, Noah, build an ark for a flood that's coming in about a hundred years." "Hey, Moses, throw down your staff and the sea will split in half."

If we relied only on human logic, we would never see God's miracles. If we follow His Word, miracles can happen.

Yes, you need to protect yourself from harm. But it is possible to serve people in a way that doesn't enable them.

As you saw in last week's reading, Luke 6:27-36 says:

> Love your enemies, do good to those who hate you, bless those who curse you, pray for those who

mistreat you. If someone slaps you on one cheek, turn to them the other also. If someone takes your coat, do not withhold your shirt from them. Give to everyone who asks you, and if anyone takes what belongs to you, do not demand it back. Do to others as you would have them do to you.

If you love those who love you, what credit is that to you? Even sinners love those who love them. And if you do good to those who are good to you, what credit is that to you? Even sinners do that. And if you lend to those from whom you expect repayment, what credit is that to you? Even sinners lend to sinners, expecting to be repaid in full. But love your enemies, do good to them, and lend to them without expecting to get anything back. Then your reward will be great, and you will be children of the Most High, because he is kind to the ungrateful and wicked. Be merciful, just as your Father is merciful.

What? Bless those who curse you, turn the other cheek, give them the shirt off your back? Why would anyone do something so preposterous? Because when you choose this path, God shows up. And He often does the opposite of what you think will happen.

Loving your "enemies" doesn't enable them, it exposes them to God's power. They will see the supernatural humility through your actions, and become convicted of their sin. You haven't said a word. You haven't lectured them, judged them, confronted them, or given them a lengthy dissertation on how wrong they've been. You simply served them.

I am not suggesting you subject yourself to physical or emotional harm. If your spouse is abusive, separate for your protection and the safety of your children. Then work on the marriage to see if God can redeem it. Find ways to serve your spouse without risking further damage. Come back under the same roof as your spouse only when it is safe to do so.

what to say

- "I feel a need to serve you better. Is there something I can help you with today?"
- "I know I tend to be selfish. I want to do what God wants me to do, which is to honor and serve you."

what to do

- Make lunch for your spouse before they leave for work.
- Say something kind to them when they walk in the door.
- Watch their favorite movie together.
- Fill up their car with gas.
- Thank them for something specific.
- Write a love letter and address it to your home or their work.
- Purchase the book *The Five Love Languages* by Gary Chapman. Read one chapter a day.

what not to do

- Don't act like your spouse's parent.
- Don't judge them or punish them. That's God's job.

what to read

- Matthew 5:43-48, 25:35-40
- Acts 20:35
- Galatians 5:13
- Hebrews 13:16

what to pray

Heavenly Father, I come to You filled with tension, conflict, and uncertainties. Serving my spouse is hard to do, and loving them is impossible on my own. I need Your Holy Spirit to empower me to speak and act toward my spouse in a way that draws them closer to me and ultimately closer to You. Help me to lean on Your abilities and let Your love flow through me. In Jesus's name, amen.

notes

_____

_____

_____

_____

_____

_____

_____

_____

_____

_____

_____

_____

_____

_____

_____

_____

_____

_____

_____

_____

_____

_____

_____

_____

_____

_____

Week 19

Serving Is Our Duty

In Matthew 20:20-28, a woman asks Jesus to place her two sons next to Him in heaven. He responds that this decision is not His to make, rather, "It's up to my Father." Then He goes on to speak about His role here on earth, and said, "the Son of Man did not come to be served, but to serve."

That had to blow their minds. They thought Jesus was the Messiah sent by God to be their King. "He wants to be a servant? And He doesn't even get to choose who sits next to Him in heaven?"

Jesus could have come to earth and demanded the honor due to Him as the Son of God, the King of Kings. Instead, He came with humility, compassion, kindness, and patience.

What if our marriage vows said, "I am not in this to be served but to serve the one I love … not just when it's convenient, or when my spouse deserves it, or when I feel like it, but at all times"? If we actually lived that way, divorce would be a rarity.

As a traveling speaker, I am well taken care of by the ministries I visit. If I'm not careful, I could start feeling entitled to such treatment and come to expect it. I must make a conscious effort to avoid the pride that can easily result from the accolades that come with my job. I am blessed to have a wife who prays for me often and lovingly reminds me that serving others is my calling.

Marriage has the same potential pitfall. If your spouse takes good care of you, you may become used to being served and start to feel entitled. It feels good to be served, and it's okay to appreciate it. But don't grow complacent or come to expect it.

The healthiest marriage is when both partners serve each other in a balanced pattern.

It's our duty as Christians to serve others, and the Lord provides blessings when we do.

what to say

- "I've been learning a lot about myself lately. I realize I haven't been a good servant to you, and I want you to know that I'm working on improving."
- "Please forgive me for not serving you the way I should."

what to do

- Bake your spouse's favorite treat.
- Take your spouse's car to get detailed.
- Compliment your spouse in front of your friends and family.
- Write an encouraging note and leave it where they will find it.
- Send a thoughtful text.
- Give your spouse a foot rub.

what to read

- Matthew 20
- Mark 10:44-45
- Philippians 2:3-4

what to pray

Dear Lord, I ask You to give me wisdom to know how to best serve my spouse during these turbulent times. Enable me to serve with a joyful heart, never keeping score, criticizing, condemning, or expecting to receive anything in return. Remind me to give of myself, my talents, my goods, and my time. Help me understand my spouse's needs. Allow me to serve my spouse as You serve, with gentleness, compassion, and tenderness. I ask this in the holy name of Jesus, amen.

notes

_____

_____

_____

_____

_____

_____

_____

_____

_____

_____

_____

_____

_____

_____

_____

_____

_____

_____

_____

_____

_____

Week 20

Serving Brings Blessings

We all want our lives to matter. We chase promotions and leadership positions because we want to make a difference. But those things won't make as much of a difference as serving.

Serving is good for the soul. When you serve others, you will experience indescribable joy and peace. Serving is also good for the mind and body, as it can ease symptoms of stress and depression. Tapping into our gifts and passions as we serve builds self-confidence, energy, and strength. Serving others can be the best distraction from our own worries.

Serving allows us to experience God's presence in new ways. As we serve others, we find ourselves feeling encouraged. That's why people who go on mission trips often come home feeling like they received more than they gave.

Serving increases our faith. As we move out of our comfort zones to serve others, God reveals new potential in ourselves. When we see what He can do when His power is at work within us, we begin looking for the doors He's opening rather than pushing our way through the one's He's closed.

Serving helps us to be more like Jesus. When we shift our focus off of ourselves onto others, we begin to see them as Jesus does. Serving is a form of worship, an opportunity to express gratitude for what Jesus has done for us, and a wonderful way to share the love and grace we've been given.

What blessings can you expect when you serve a spouse who may be undeserving and ungrateful? Take a look at how Luke 6:32-36 reads in the Great News Bible:

> If you love only the people who love you, *why should you receive a blessing?* Even sinners love those who love them! And if you do good only to those who do good to you, *why should you receive a blessing?* Even sinners do that! And if you lend only to those from whom you hope to get it back, why should you receive a blessing? Even sinners lend to sinners, to get back the same amount! No! *Love your enemies and do good to them; lend and expect nothing back. You will then have a great reward, and you will be children of the Most High God. For he is good to the ungrateful and the wicked. Be merciful just as your Father is merciful.*

Three times Jesus asks, "Why should you receive a blessing for doing good to someone who is good to you?" He then describes the blessings that will fall upon you if you do good to someone who is undeserving: we become the children of the Most High God. He calls this a "great reward." Being a Christian means loving the unlovable with the supernatural power of the Holy Spirit, which was put in you at salvation.

Jesus goes on to say that God is good to the ungrateful and the wicked. He reminds us that we are wicked and ungrateful too. But when we serve those around us who don't deserve it, God gives us favor, mercy, and blessings.

I want to challenge you to serve your spouse like never before and see what God does in and through you. There is no guarantee that the person you are serving will change. But God will bless your effort.

what to say

- Every day this week, ask, "What's one specific thing I can do for you, or take off your plate today?"

what to do

- Choose to be happy and positive.
- Surprise your spouse at work and take them out to lunch.
- Send your spouse an email just to say, "Thanks!"
- Say, "I love you," more often.
- Make your spouse breakfast or coffee before work.
- Get your spouse's favorite magazine and have it delivered to their work to say, "I'm thinking of you."

what to read

- Psalm 1:1-3, 23:1-4
- 2 Corinthians 9:8
- Colossians 3:23-24

what to pray

Lord, You sent Your Son to give His life for me. What a blessing! Let Your Spirit awaken that same spirit of service within me. Help me to be meek and humble so I can serve my spouse willfully, obediently, and faithfully, even when it hurts. I trust Your blessings will follow and I'll be able to withstand our relational tension and to grow closer to my spouse. In Jesus's name, amen.

notes

in sickness and
in health

Week 21

Your Vows Matter

Think back to your wedding day. What's the first thing that comes to mind? The ceremony, the reception, your guests, the wedding party? How about your vows? Do you remember them well enough to recite them now?

It not, don't feel bad. Most people can't recall what they said in their wedding vows.

When I married my wife, we used the traditional vows, which include the phrase "to have and to hold, from this day forward, for better, for worse, for richer, for poorer, in sickness and in health, to love and to cherish, till death do us part, according to God's holy ordinance." I must confess, when I stood at the altar and made those promises, I didn't think much about the "worse" or the "sickness" part. I only thought of the bliss that lay ahead of us, as my beautiful bride and I spent the rest of our lives together.

Whether you went with traditional wording or wrote your own, vows are not meant to be merely a collection of words you say once and then forget. They represent a solemn covenant between you, your spouse, and God.

Mark 10:9 (NASB) says, "What therefore God has joined together, let no man separate." Genesis 2:24 says, "That is why a man leaves his father and mother and is united to his wife, and they become one flesh." God created marriage, and He placed countless passages in the Bible for us to follow in order to honor that creed. Unfortunately, many couples disregard those passages when times get tough.

In any marriage, feelings of love may fade from time to time. That's not what keeps couples together. When emotions turn negative, the vows you made can keep you together long enough for the positive feelings to return.

If your wedding vows really only meant "We'll stay married as long as we're happy," there's no promise in that statement. God meant for marriage to be a commitment between two people for life. If we end up in a situation where we need to lean on God to get through the day, He can get you through. If you focus more on God and less on yourself, your marriage can improve and thrive.

The deepest level of love can be formed when couples endure hardships, failures, and betrayals. Their true selves are unveiled, with all their flaws, yet they choose to remain together in spite of the hurt and pain.

At one point you loved your spouse enough to marry them. So while you may want to travel back in time to your wedding day, and tell your past self what to *really* expect from marriage, you don't need to. You can have a fresh start today, *from this day forward.*

what to say

- "I take our marriage vows seriously and am honored to pour myself into this marriage and give it my all."
- "I made a vow to you and I intend to keep it. I'm in this for the long haul."

what to do

- Write out the vows you took when you got married and keep them handy as you pray. Ask God to give you and your spouse the strength to fulfill those vows.
- Pray for your spouse every day.
- Focus on changing yourself, not your spouse.
- Meet your spouse's most important emotional need.
- Visit refreshyourmarriage.org to get connected with a certified mentor couple who can help you.

what to read

- Genesis 2:18-24
- Malachi 2:16
- Mark 10:11-12
- Luke 16:18
- Romans 7:2
- 1 Corinthians 7:39
- Hebrews 13:4

what to pray

Dear Father God, You have given mankind the beautiful gift of marriage. And You fulfilled the desire of my heart the day I got married. You've seen when we failed to live according to Your ideals, and we now find ourselves in a broken relationship. Help us to be willing to accept our own responsibility in this and be willing to ask for forgiveness and to extend forgiveness. May we never retaliate when we feel wronged. Help us to make choices that will show that we have made a commitment of love to You and to each other. May joy, peace, and contentment dwell within us as we strive to rebuild our marriage. May the devotion we declared in our marriage vows be restored to a radiant reflection of Your love for us. I ask this in the name of Jesus, amen.

notes

Week 22

Trust in God's Power

Are you tired? Worn out? Lonely? Sad? Feeling like there's nowhere to turn? God understands. He wants to be your rock.

God created the heavens and the earth. He created a great flood that destroyed the world, then He rebuilt it with a chosen family. He parted the Red Sea to allow the Israelites to escape their captors. God's Son raised the dead, made the blind see, and enabled the lame to walk. Is there any doubt that He can turn your situation around for your good and His glory?

Satan has tricked many people into believing that God's power isn't real. "If He was real, He wouldn't let bad things happen to good people." The truth is, according to His Word, God has unlimited power and infinite knowledge.

You may wonder if your relationship will ever change. But don't let your frustration get the best of you. While you and your spouse's best efforts may fail, God will never fail you.

You are powerless to control or change your spouse. If you've come to the place where you realize that all the strategies you've tried have failed, make God the focus of your life. Not yourself, your spouse, your children, your career. Leave your spouse in God's hands and trust His power to work in your marriage. Whatever condition your marriage is in, God can perform miracles, transform lives, and heal broken hearts.

Fully subject yourself to God and His power. Allow God to show Himself in your marriage and your family. He is able to transform your heart and your situation. The key is to trust in His timing and allow Him to work in and through you.

The power of God can bring hope, courage, and new life to even the darkest days. Ask God to give you a new life in Him. Then live according to His mighty power.

what to say

- "I believe in God's power to change us and our marriage."
- "I believe in God's Word and trust Him to transform both of us to bring Him glory."

what to do

- Journal your prayers. Reread them after some time has gone by and make note of which ones got answered.
- Make a list of ways that you have experienced God's mighty power in your life.
- Remain fervent in reading God's Word to stay encouraged.

what to read

- Genesis 18:14
- Exodus 13:9
- Job 11:7
- Psalm 78:12-16
- Mark 10:27
- Luke 1:37
- 2 Corinthians 10:4
- Ephesians 1:18-21

what to pray

Heavenly Father, I believe You have the power to heal my marriage. You demonstrated your power throughout biblical history and you continue to reveal Your power in miraculous ways today. Even when my faith is weak, my love for You is strong. I know You hold my life in Your hands and that Your grace is sufficient for me. I want Your will to be my will. In Jesus's name, amen.

notes

Week 23

We Are All Flawed

When I look into the depths of my soul, I see a man who is far from perfect. I have flaws and imperfections. The woman I married, while beautiful on the outside, has internal flaws and imperfections as well. But because I love her, I accept her as she is. That is unconditional love.

Many people have a hard time recognizing their own flaws, but are quick to see the flaws in others.

If you have been wounded and can't release those who have wounded you, you are focusing too much on your circumstances and not enough on God. Do you carry a list in your heart of all the wrongs your spouse has committed? When you get into a fight, do you refer to that list in order to accuse your spouse and justify yourself?

In Matthew 7:3-5 Jesus asked His listeners, "Why do you look at the speck of sawdust in your brother's eye and pay no attention to the plank in your own eye? ...First take the plank out of your own eye, and then you will see clearly to remove the speck from your brother's eye."

When people are going through difficult circumstances, such as a marriage with problems, there's a tendency to focus only on the challenges. Too much time is spent trying to change their spouse, that it can be easy to neglect other areas of life.

While you're doing your best to work on your marriage, don't forget about how you can bless and be blessed by friends, loved ones, church family, even strangers. Make time in your life for friendships and for ministries where you can find fulfillment and make a difference in other people's lives. Many times when we serve, God ministers to our own pain.

what to say

- "After some soul-searching, I've realized that I have been so focused on your shortcomings that I was blind to my own. I'm sorry for that. Please be patient with me as I continue to find ways to be a better spouse."

what to do

- Identify areas of your life where you may be too self-focused. Be honest with yourself. Consider your relationships with your children, coworkers, friends, neighbors, etc.

- The next time you are with someone, spend more time asking what's going on in their life and less time talking about yourself.

- When you have critical thoughts about a person, remind yourself, "I am imperfect, flawed, and desperate for God's mercy."

- Find ways to serve others. Perhaps help out at a food pantry or retirement home. Focusing on others will help you focus less on yourself. It will also make your life more rewarding and enjoyable.

- Pick one thing your spouse normally does around the house (cleaning, cooking, yard work, taking out the garbage, pet clean-up) and do it for them without them asking.

what to read

- Matthew 7
- Romans 12
- 1 Corinthians 13:4-5

what to pray

Lord, You've told me in scripture to come to You and ask for every need of life. Since You are the God who heals, I pray for healing for my spouse and for myself. I pray that we get the help we need—physically, emotionally, and spiritually. I'm coming to You today as Your child, longing to hear from You and asking for Your divine healing in me, in my spouse, and in our marriage. In Jesus's name, amen.

notes

_____
_____
_____
_____
_____
_____
_____
_____
_____
_____
_____
_____
_____
_____
_____
_____
_____
_____

Week 24

Give God a Chance

Jenny followed the path in this book up to week twenty. She was respectful toward her husband. She'd repented of her own part in the problems. She'd been supportive of her husband, patient with him. She forgave him. Essentially, she followed this plan to the letter. Yet she saw no change in her husband. He was still distant.

"This isn't working," she shouted in her kitchen one day, exhausted and hopeless. "Where is God in all this?"

Perhaps you feel the same way.

Let's take a step back and get a fresh perspective on your journey so far.

Is it possible there have been some small positive steps along the way that you haven't noticed? Your ability to walk this path is a miracle in itself.

If you have children, they are learning how to face their own trials by watching you face this one. Because of your faithfulness in this quest, your children will grow up seeing God's power. Even if you are the only one who is transformed in this marriage, your children will be mightily blessed by your example.

God has been with you, and He has given you strength and courage. He is still there. And He is proud of you.

The Bible tells a story about the prophet Elijah, who performed a great miracle when he confronted King Ahab about his worship of false gods. Following specific divine instructions, Elijah built an altar to the one true God. Then he challenged King Ahab and the king's four hundred prophets to build an altar next to his, saying that the real God would breathe down fire from heaven and burn up the offering.

With thousands of people watching, King Ahab's four hundred prophets built their altar alongside Elijah's. They prayed to their gods. Nothing happened. They prayed more. Still nothing. "Pray louder," Elijah suggested with a laugh. "Maybe your god is sleeping or taking a break."

Elijah then prayed to God, and fire came down from heaven and consumed his altar with amazing force. All the people fell to their knees. The false prophets were then seized and killed.

In just the next chapter, we find Elijah running to the hills in fear that he would be captured and killed by King Ahab and his wife, Jezebel. While Elijah was crouched down and hiding, God spoke out loud to him, asking, "What are you doing here?"

Essentially, God was saying, "I have shown you My power, My protection, and My ability to go before you and lay out a path for you. I created the foundations of the universe. And after all that, you run and hide in fear of your enemy. What are you doing?"

I want to ask you the same question. If you're feeling fearful or hopeless, consider what God has already done for you, what He has already shown you. Has He not proven His power and His love for you?

Remain bold in Him and His promises. Stay true to the path He put before you. Stay on this quest. Give God a chance to pour out His power. He will.

God has promised that He will always be there for you. He will never leave you. He loves you. Let Him fill you up.

God created marriage, and He knows how hard it can be at times. Cry out to Him. Lean on Him. Ask Him to feed you, to fill you, to give you peace and joy.

If you're not getting your needs met in your marriage, turn to God and say, "I need to feel loved. I need to feel special." Ask Him to meet those needs. Take some time for yourself when you need to rejuvenate. Ask God to help you find ways to carve that time into your schedule.

Marriage is never supposed to replace God. He is to be your primary need.

what to say (to Yourself)

- "I will remain faithful to my spouse; no matter how hard things get."
- "I trust in my God and His power."
- "I choose to see the miracles God has already performed for me and trust in the miracles He has prepared for me."

what to do

- Visualize your fear and hopelessness as being like the cave where Elijah was hiding. Then imagine yourself coming out of it and continuing on your quest.
- Keep your focus on the goal, which is honoring the Lord God.
- Continue loving and respecting your spouse, even in the face of rejection.
- Set aside some time each day to unplug from technology and focus on your spouse.
- Make a lunch for your spouse every day this week before they leave for work.

what not to do

- Don't give up.
- Don't fall back into old patterns.
- Don't use the word *divorce* in your conversations.
- Don't pull away from your spouse and shut down.
- Don't turn to nonbelievers or people of the opposite sex for emotional support.

what to read

- 1 Kings 18-21
- Psalm 139:13-14
- Jeremiah 32:27
- Matthew 17:20, 21:21
- Mark 10:27

what to pray

Lord, I don't always know what Your will is, especially in times like this, but I desperately seek Your face. I bow before You to tell You the desire of my heart: to spend as many years as I can loving you, loving others, and becoming more like You. But whatever you choose to accomplish in my life is up to You—and okay with me. You deserve all the praise. In the powerful name of Jesus, amen.

notes

_____
_____
_____
_____
_____
_____
_____
_____

affirm and encourage

Week 25

Discover Areas to Affirm

One of the most effective ways to help your spouse is to offer encouraging words. According to Webster's Dictionary, the word *encourage* means "to inspire courage." All of us have areas in which we feel insecure, and a lack of courage often hinders us from accomplishing the things we would like to do.

Positive words not only encourage us; they also motivate us. If a man fails to get a promotion at work, he may feel like a failure. But when his wife says, "You're still important to me," he finds the courage to work through his disappointment and is motivated to move forward.

Most of us have more potential than we will ever develop. The thing that holds us back is often a lack of courage. A wife may want to enroll in an educational course to develop her potential in a subject she's passionate about. Encouraging words from her husband may supply the courage she needs to take that first step.

Everyone appreciates receiving words of affirmation. They can come through letters, text messages, phone calls, emails or face-to-face. The content is more important than the mode of delivery.

When someone praises you, you want to repeat the behavior that brought about that praise, right? That's human nature. If the praise isn't genuine, it can be a form of manipulation. But when it's authentic, it can be a powerful way to motivate others.

This works the opposite way too. You'll get more of what you complain about if you focus on the negative and point it out all the time. In all of your relationships, it pays to be positive. Notice the good things and affirm them. That will reinforce the positive behavior and cause it to occur more often.

If you're in a rough patch in your marriage, you might have a hard time seeing your spouse's good qualities. But I promise, they're there! Maybe your spouse is really brave or kind or considerate or perseverant. Is he or she a great cook, a great provider, a nurturer? Wise at managing money? Whatever these qualities may be, affirm them and they'll get stronger.

Harvard Business Review posted a research report stating that humans need a five-to-one ratio of affirmation to criticism.[3] After reading this, I kept track of how many critical statements and how many positive statements I made in one day. I have never considered myself a pessimist, but the results indicated that I might be!

When I travel, my wife sometimes puts notes in my luggage. That means so much to me. A few weeks ago, she left a note on the mirror in our bathroom that said, "Honey, I am so thankful that you worked in the yard this weekend. Thank you for making our home a safe place." It made me want to do even more for her.

Are you giving your spouse five affirming comments to every critical one? Or has your criticism over the years chipped away at their heart, which is now as hard as concrete? Maybe your spouse has done that to you. Affirmation can be a powerful step toward a healthier relationship.

what to say

- "I am so thankful that you ..."

- "It really means a lot to me when you ..."
- "I appreciate how you ..."
- "I love seeing your quality of _____ in our children."
- "I wish I could _____ the way you do."
- "I'm proud of you for ..."

what to do

- Plan to offer words of affirmation every day.
- Strive to offer a 5:1 ratio of affirmation vs. criticism to your spouse and kids.
- Write ten words you would use to describe your spouse's character and give them the list.
- Send your spouse a text message that expresses your gratitude for something specific.

what to read

- 2 Chronicles 10:7
- Job 4:4
- Proverbs 16:24; 31:26

what to pray

Dear Lord, thank You for creating me and my spouse and for bringing us together. Thank You for giving us worth in Your eyes. Help us live as the people you uniquely intended us to be. I know my spouse has a lot to offer in this relationship, but I tend to be blinded by my pain and my own issues. Help me to see the good in my spouse and not focus on the bad. In Jesus's name, amen.

notes

Week 26

Be Strategic

You know how important it is to say, "I love you," to your spouse. But while those words are powerful, sometimes they aren't enough. Hearing *why* someone loves you can make you feel like you're in heaven.

Written notes and emails are terrific ways to affirm someone, but saying how you feel in person carries extra power because you can use body language and facial expressions. You can touch and hold each other while you deliver those powerful words. The light in your eyes can speak louder than your words.

Catch your spouse doing something that pleases you and say, "*That's* why I love you." Or ask, "Do you know what I like about you?" and then follow up with your reasons. It could be the way they make you laugh, or the way they interact with your children, or the way they attempt to serve you. You don't have to be a poet, but try to express a sense of wonder and delight. The delivery is nearly as important as the message.

Take advantage of humorous and lighthearted moments to say a few simple words of affirmation, such as, "I love the way you laugh," or, "I love that you bring humor to our relationship."

Affirming your spouse will have great dividends for you. Each time you give your spouse loving words, you're saying, "I value you." They feel treasured and adored. But something even more amazing happens when you sincerely express appreciation for your spouse: their value goes up in your eyes too. You see them the way you are describing them. And love grows.

Criticism may be your natural go-to strategy. If your spouse shares a desire or opinion, do you always express an opposing view?

Next time the voice of opposition comes into your head, before it comes out of your mouth and into your spouse's ear, ask yourself, "Is it really necessary for me to share this? Is it helpful?" If the answer is yes, speak your mind. But you don't have to voice your opinion every time.

A spouse who is constantly criticized will begin to think, *I guess I can't do anything right.* Feeling unloved and disrespected, they will respond with more criticism or withdraw completely.

If it is necessary, criticism should be given sparingly, at the right time, with the intention of being productive, and wrapped with encouragement.

When you try to control your situation, you are taking it out of God's hands. Give it back to Him. He's got this.

what to say

- Share with your spouse three reasons you chose to marry them.
- "I believe in you because ..."
- "It impressed me when you ..."
- "I'll always stand by you."
- "Being your spouse is an honor."

what to do

- Honestly evaluate your pattern of criticism and begin to be more positive.

- Focus on the goodness of your spouse.
- Buy your spouse their favorite treat at the grocery store.
- Call your spouse just to say hi.
- Hold hands with your spouse while watching TV.
- Write notes giving specific reasons you love and appreciate your spouse and put them in various locations for your spouse to see (car, bathroom, fridge, office, computer, etc.).

what to read

- *Love & Respect* by Dr. Emerson Eggerichs
- Proverbs 21:19; 27:15
- Ephesians 5:33

what to pray

Father God, thank You for the clarity to see how love protects relationships. Help me to protect those I care about by loving them. Give me wisdom and discernment in knowing how to win back my spouse. I pray this in Jesus's name, amen.

notes

_____
_____
_____
_____
_____
_____
_____
_____
_____
_____
_____
_____

Week 27

Be Authentic

What if the only positive thing your spouse could think of to say to you was "You vacuum really well"? You would be crushed!

Everyone has special abilities, gifts, talents, and skills. We all have personality and character strengths too.

Identify your spouse's strengths. Tell them how their positive attributes make you feel. Praise their ability to handle money and how that makes you feel secure and well taken care of. Tell them how proud you are when they sing or play an instrument, or when they repair a car. Or when they react in a patient, thoughtful manner to an irritating situation.

Nobody's opinion impacts you more than that of your spouse. Your opinion of them deeply impacts their self-image too. Ultimately, our self-image should be shaped by Jesus. We can all be confident and bold about who we are in Him. But human nature comes with a desire to feel affirmed and valued by others.

Make sure your words of affirmation are sincere, and not something to check off your to-do list. Take the time to think about What to say to your spouse and ensure that it is honest, specific, and deserved.

If you can't find anything genuinely complimentary to say about your spouse, look harder. You could start with something simple, like "You look great in that dress" or "I appreciate how you spoke to our son when he was acting disrespectful," or "Thanks for taking out the garbage." Eventually, this will become a natural habit in your daily conversation.

what to say

- "I feel blessed to have you in my life."
- "I'm so glad you chose me."
- "I admire the way you …"
- "You really look good in that ..."
- "I love you, need you, and want you."
- If it seems like the right time, seek a third party for help. Contact your church or contact us at daretobedifferent. com.

what to do

- Make sure your affirmations are true. Don't overdo the amplitude or frequency.
- Handwrite a letter expressing genuine, heartfelt love and admiration.
- See to it that words of encouragement are the first words your spouse hears from you in the morning and the last words they hear from you at night.
- Text your spouse a song, poem, or quote and say, "I read/ listened to this today and thought of you/us."

what to read

- Proverbs 3:27
- Romans 12:9, 13:7
- James 3:17

what to pray

God, You know me so well. You created me. You know the number of hairs on my head, and You know the thoughts in my heart before they are spoken. As I attempt to draw my spouse closer to me, I pray that my thoughts and words will come from a heart that is righteous and holy. Help my spouse to see my efforts to restore our marriage as authentic and pure, and not just a way to get what I want. Help them to see me through Your eyes and to trust You during these turbulent times. I ask this in Jesus's name, amen.

notes

_____

_____

_____

_____

_____

_____

_____

_____

_____

_____

_____

_____

_____

_____

_____

_____

_____

_____

_____

_____

_____

_____

Week 28

Be Consistent

What we say matters, but how we say it matters even more. Consistency is the most important key when it comes to encouragement and affirmation for your spouse.

Most people aren't naturally affirming. We have to fight our critical nature and habitual tendencies.

In a mentoring session I had with a woman, she complained to me about the affirmation her husband gave her, saying, "He only praised me because you told him to."

I asked her, "Did he mean it?" When she answered yes, I asked, "So what's the problem?" It's okay to schedule kindness. Prayer. Sex. Quality time. If something is good for your family, plan for it. Especially if it does not naturally become the priority that it should.

what to say

- "I'm glad you're my friend."
- "When you listened to me, you made me feel valued."
- "I'm a better person because of you."

- "I want to grow old with you."
- "God has my best in mind, which is why He gave me you."
- "You will always have my heart."
- "You have a lot to offer."

what to do

- Schedule daily words of affirmation on your calendar.
- Share a favorite family memory with your spouse.
- Take a fun selfie together and post it on your social media, including words affirming your spouse.
- Encourage your spouse with a scripture.
- Bring your spouse their morning coffee.
- Say something nice about your spouse in front of others.
- Include your children, coworkers, family, and friends in your affirmation process.

what to read

- Romans 14:19
- 2 Corinthians 13:11
- Ephesians 4:2
- 2 Timothy 1:7
- James 5:12

what to pray

Heavenly Father, thank You for your guidance. Help me to be consistent in showing my love for my spouse. Forgive me for getting ahead of Your plans, and help me know when to stop and listen for Your direction. Your ways are perfect, Lord. Thank You for offering Your gentle grace. In Jesus's name, amen.

notes

guard your heart

Week 29

Protect Your Heart from Bitterness

Guarding your heart can be one of the greatest challenges you will face.

Hebrews 3:13 tells us to encourage one another daily so our hearts won't grow hardened. Feelings of loneliness, anger, stress, lust, or hopelessness can lead to despair. Sin can twist an honest feeling into a web of self-justification and choices that lead you down a dead-end road. Bitterness is often the result, and it produces such heartbreaks as alcohol addiction, drug dependency, affairs, and depression.

There is no medication to remedy bitterness. Drugs only numb the pain and leave you wanting more.

When your heart grows hard toward a person, even if you have justification, a shield forms around it. That shield may offer some protection from further harm, but it also blocks your heart from the Lord and His followers.

Be honest about your feelings, but don't embrace them for too long. Take your pain to the Lord. He is your strength and your refuge. He has the answers to your agony and the remedy for your pain. Matthew 11:28-30 tells us to cast our burdens and our anxiety upon the Lord. He will be your healing ointment and your compass during the dark hours and offer you rest.

Satan and his demons can enter your life through the root of bitterness. Fight it with all your might! Forgive, and let God avenge you.

what to say (to your children)

- "Continue loving your mom/dad no matter what."
- "Let's keep a very special place in our hearts for your mom/dad."
- "God loves your mom/dad so much. Continue praying for her/him."

what to do

- Share any bitter thoughts with your accountability partner, small group, or Christian counselor.
- Repent often.
- Forgive often (including yourself).
- Keep thinking of the end goal: to glorify God.
- Journal your thoughts and feelings. Include something positive for each day.
- Live in the present. Set small goals for yourself each day.

what to read

- Psalm 55:22
- Proverbs 4:23
- Matthew 11:28-30
- Romans 12:19
- Hebrews 3:13, 12:14-15
- 1 Peter 5:7

what to pray

Lord, I ask You to protect my mind and heart. Set my mind on You. Transform me by the renewing of my mind so that I may prove what Your will is: that which is good and acceptable and perfect. Help me, by the power of Your Spirit, to think about whatever is true, honorable, right, pure, lovely, excellent, and worthy of praise. In Jesus's name, amen.

notes

_____
_____
_____
_____
_____
_____
_____
_____
_____
_____
_____
_____
_____
_____
_____
_____
_____
_____
_____
_____
_____
_____
_____

Week 30

Protect Your Heart from Loneliness

Humans are not meant to live in isolation. We all crave deep and lasting connections with other people. We marry with the hope that our spouse will be a lifelong companion who saves us from loneliness. Over time, however, couples can gradually disconnect and withdraw from each other.

If you're feeling isolated, chances are your spouse is too. Take the first step to reconnecting with them, even if it's a small gesture. Open up to them about how you feel and give them an opportunity to do the same.

If you have been feeling alone for a long time, hurts have likely been building up. If you have been wronged, make the decision to forgive your spouse. And if you have wounded them, seek their forgiveness.

Sometimes couples get so busy, so caught up in their individual lives or in their children's lives, that they neglect to spend time together. Communication fades to surface talk or nothing at all. Be pro-active. Initiate time together with your spouse. Do things that are fun and inspiring. Be creative. Surprise your spouse with a well-planned getaway they will enjoy. Plan date nights, walks, and coffee-shop moments.

If you are rejected, try again in a few days. Change your approach. Try something less complicated. Success is often the result of repeated failures.

Loneliness can fuel thoughts and actions that end up destroying a marriage and a family. Affairs result from unattended issues that built up over months, sometimes years. An emotional affair often leads to a sexual one. Either way, infidelity can be devastating.

An affair isn't the only replacement for loneliness. Porn, alcohol, drugs, spending money, and social media addiction are others. Acknowledge your lonely feelings and create a strategy to alleviate them in a God-honoring way rather than a self-destructive and sinful way.

Galatians 6:2 encourages us to share each other's burdens. Create a healthy emotional support network of friends and family members. Try not to overwhelm them with your woes. And don't throw your spouse under the bus. Simply let your support team encourage you and lift you up.

Let your loneliness push you toward your spouse, not away from them. God will give you courage and comfort along the way.

what to say

- "Can I cook dinner tonight or give you a back rub?"
- "I'd like to get away with you for the weekend. Let's tune out the world and do an overnight trip somewhere."
- "Can we turn off the TV tonight and play a board game?"

what to do

- Open up to your spouse about how you feel and give them an opportunity to do the same.
- Schedule a date night (in or out).
- Sit close to each other, give your spouse a neck massage, and surprise them with a kiss.

what not to do

- Don't fantasize about someone else.
- Don't go on social media looking for friendships with the opposite sex.
- Don't share your pain with the opposite sex.
- Don't dabble with porn.

what to read

- Psalm 147:3
- Isaiah 41:10
- 1 Corinthians 10:13

what to pray

Lord, my heart is broken, but You are near. My spirit is crushed, but You are my rescuer. Your word is my hope. It revives me and comforts me, especially when I'm lonely. You are the breath of life within me. You are my help, the one who sustains me. I am weak, but You are strong. I trust You to rescue me from this dark cloud of despair because You delight in me. In Jesus's name, amen.

notes

_____

_____

_____

_____

_____

_____

_____

_____

_____

_____

_____

Week 31

Protect Your Heart From Entitlement

"I don't deserve to be treated like this. I'm the good spouse." Ever felt that way? It's called entitlement.

Contrary to the world's perspective, marriage isn't just about your happiness. None of us are entitled to anything. Every breath we've been given is only by the grace of God. We're all sinners, and all we *deserve* is separation from God, some call it *hell*. But praise God; He saved us from that fate.

One of the most powerful ways we can honor the Lord in our marriage is to die to our selfishness, love each other as Christ loved us, and be thankful for all God has given us.

In marriage, entitlement breeds reciprocation. "If I do this for him, he'll do that for me." Don't expect your spouse to always reciprocate your feelings and actions. The truth is, people are different. We're raised differently, we understand situations differently, and we give and receive love differently. It's not as simple as "Hey, we're married now, so I deserve to be loved, obeyed, and happy." With that mindset, when your expectations for being loved or obeyed or happy aren't met, you become bitter and angry.

At the root of almost all marriage problems is unmet expectations.

When things don't go the way we anticipated, we have two options: One is to try to figure out what we need to do to get our spouse to meet our expectations. The other option is to realize that we have no right to expect anything from anybody, including God, and that anything we have received is an undeserved gift. One of these options leads to a lifetime of disappointment, disillusionment, and frustration. The other leads to freedom, peace, and gratitude.

In a good marriage, each partner is striving to give 100 percent effort, all the time. If I decide I'm only going to put in an equal amount of effort as my spouse, I'll spend most of my time keeping score. That's only going to result in you feeling frustrated. Compounded over many years, it could turn into a lifetime of resentment.

No one can give 100 percent all the time. We all have bad days. My wife could be operating at 20 percent one day, then pouring 100 percent into our marriage the next day. I can't control what she does. I can only control what I do. My desire is to strive for 100 percent as often as possible so I'm honoring the one who's at the center of our marriage: God.

Try being the better spouse in God's eyes. It's one of the best ways you can honor God in the role He has blessed you with.

what to say

- "I want to always serve you without expecting anything in return. Will you forgive me for the times when I've felt entitled?"

- "I truly appreciate you and all the good you bring to our relationship."

- "Is there anything I can do that would make your day easier?"

- "I want you to know that I'm willing to give one hundred percent to this marriage."

what to do

- Search your heart and then journal about areas where you may feel entitled. Repent for those areas of entitlement.
- Start performing acts of kindness for your spouse for the simple pleasure of serving them—not to get anything in return. Try to incorporate into each day one small way to serve them.
- Watch what your spouse wants to watch on TV.
- Remember what you deserve from God for your sin and selfishness, and thank Him for His mercy and grace.

what to read

- Romans 8
- Galatians 6:5
- Colossians 3:23
- James 4:1-12, 17

what to pray

Lord, help me not to lean on my own understanding but in everything acknowledge You so that You can direct my words, thoughts, and actions. Father, take away any feelings of entitlement that may have crept into my heart and replace those thoughts with humility, purity, and integrity so my character reflects that of Christ. In Jesus's name, amen.

notes

_____
_____
_____
_____
_____
_____

Week 32

Protect Your Heart from Indifference

A great marriage doesn't happen by accident. No one accidentally becomes a loving spouse or develops deep intimacy in their marriage.

Every great accomplishment in life requires two things: precision and effort.

When we don't have precision or effort in our relationship with our spouse, with God, or in our career, we start to lose ground. That neglected area of our life begins to fade, like a flower without sunshine or rain.

Often times a broken marriage exists because we don't make "together time" a priority. Unless we deliberately work on this, it's rarely going to happen.

Pam and I schedule weekly date nights on our calendar, just like we schedule meetings, deadlines, and other important events. We make time for each other a priority.

Another important priority when building a strong marriage is to pursue God. Matthew 6:33 (ESV) tells us, "Seek first the kingdom of God and his righteousness, and all these things will be added to you." The more we seek God, the more we are filled by His love and grace and the more we will want to become vessels of that love to our spouses.

Indifference can sometimes be useful. Doctors, nurses, and paramedics need to remain indifferent or they could induce fear into their patients. This may come across as uncaring, but it is simply professionalism. Those who have worked in emergency care for years may seem insulated to trauma, even calloused. But I'd rather have an indifferent doctor than one who screams, "He's going to die! God help us all!"

However, indifference can't exist in a family unit without causing damage. Children need to feel a sense of security from their parents. Wives need to feel an emotional connection to their husbands. Husbands need to feel appreciated and respected.

The quest you're on requires you to give your heart to your spouse over and over while putting your trust in the Lord. He will heal you and give you strength as He works through you supernaturally.

God asks us to love those who hate and mistreat us. He challenges us to give more to those who steal our belongings. He asks us to turn the other cheek and continue to engage with people who wound us. His promise is to be our doctor, our surgeon, our nurse, and our caretaker.

Fight the urge to be indifferent. Stay present in the fight so God can work through you to reach your spouse.

what to say

- "I'm sorry if I've been insensitive. I want to give you my whole heart and hold back nothing. I'm trusting God to help me with this."
- "I feel like we've become complacent in our marriage. What can I do to revive the magic in our relationship?"

what to do

- Search your heart and then journal about any feelings (good or bad) that you may be experiencing.
- Choose to love your spouse. Express that love with words or actions, speaking their *love language*. (*The Five Love Languages* by Gary Chapman was recommended in Week 18).
- Become a boyfriend or girlfriend all over again. Write down the things you did that won their heart in the first place.
- Plan a thoughtful gesture. She may want a walk and deep relational connection, talking about dreams and passions. He may want to take a road trip with some favorite music bringing back memories. If that's what they like, that's what you need to do.
- Step into your partner's point of view. Attempt to view things from their perspective, even if you disagree with it or believe it's wrong. What new information does that give you?

what to read

- Joshua 1:9
- Proverbs 3:5-6
- Luke 6:45

what to pray

I come before You, Lord, to ask for Your blessing on my marriage. Help my spouse and me to come together in harmony, with sympathy, compassion, humility, faithfulness, honesty, respect, and love. Lord, You have made us one in flesh and spirit, and You are a witness to our marriage covenant. I believe that the Holy Spirit is working in our marriage so that neither of us will be deceived by the persuasive words of anyone who might lead us astray. Help me to always remember that You are in control. I trust Your will to be done. In Jesus's name, amen.

notes

_____
_____
_____
_____
_____
_____
_____
_____
_____
_____
_____
_____
_____
_____
_____
_____
_____
_____
_____
_____
_____
_____
_____
_____
_____
_____
_____
_____

endure through
the storm

Week 33

Think Long Term

Great relationships are predicated on long-term faithfulness. Time is not just a great healer; it also provides the space we need to work things out. Even a "difficult" marriage can be a good marriage. The best relationships involve challenges.

If your spouse is responding well to your efforts in this process so far, praise God! But marriage is a lifelong journey, so don't let up on the gas if you're starting to see some momentum.

A few years ago, I was helping a friend whose wife had left him for another lover. I asked him, "What do you feel God is telling you to do?"

He answered, "Forgive her and fight for her."

I told him I would help him. We drafted up a love letter in which he accepted his personal blame for their broken marriage and promised to wait for her to return to him.

Months after he sent that letter, God answered his prayers and created a wedge between her and her lover, which ultimately led her back to the Lord. And to her husband. They rededicated their lives to each other and to God.

Pam and I ran into them recently. They were walking arm-in-arm and looked like they were filled with joy. Their journey to get to that point was riddled with loneliness, anger, betrayal, lies, deceit, and abuse. But the dark days of their marriage were the catalyst to their wake-up call. God used their pain and struggles to help them find healing, spiritually and relationally.

Obviously, I would never condone having an affair. But the pain of infidelity often forces spouses to evaluate what really matters and what's worth fighting for.

Many people finally turn to Christ when they're are at the bottom of the valley, in utter desperation. That is where we take a good look at ourselves, our marriages, and our purpose in life.

what to say

- "I am committed to you and to this marriage."
- "I am hopeful that if we put God first, He will help us endure."
- Say "thank you" for the little things.
- Avoid phrases like "You always ..." or "You never ...."

what to do

- Remind your partner that you appreciate them.
- Be kind in the midst of your pain.
- Practice letting go of offenses.
- Forgive often.
- Make a list of all the reasons you married your spouse.

what to read

- Genesis 50:20
- Romans 5
- Hebrews 10
- James 1:2-3

what to pray

Holy Lord, thank You for Your grace. Please help me move beyond the hurdles that trip me up, and give me the strength and wisdom to see the hope that can be found only in Christ. No matter what happens in the future or the outcome of our marriage, I need a deep-down cleansing and strengthening—a wholehearted renewal of all that I am, because all that I am is Yours. Use this trial to strengthen me from a "what-if" faith to a "no-matter-what" faith. In all things I choose to honor You and give You glory. In Jesus's name, amen.

notes

_____

_____

_____

_____

_____

_____

_____

_____

_____

_____

_____

_____

_____

_____

_____

_____

_____

_____

_____

Week 34

Count the Cost of Divorce

Many years ago, the myth began to circulate that if parents are unhappy, the kids are unhappy too. So divorce could help both parent and child. "What's good for mom or dad is good for the children," it was assumed. But we now have an enormous amount of research on divorce and children, all pointing to the same truth: Kids suffer when moms and dads split up. And it turns out divorce doesn't make mom and dad happier, either.

When couples are considering whether or not to work through their marital issues, they rarely calculate the true cost of divorce. If they did, they might reconsider. So let me reveal some of the hidden costs.

Here are some statistics compiled by Larry Bilotta at marriage-success-secrets.com.

Children and Divorce

Studies show that children who've lived through multiple divorces earn lower grades and their peers rate them as being less pleasant to be around.[4]

Teenagers in single-parent families and blended families are three times more likely to need psychological help within a given year.[5]

Children from homes disrupted by divorce have more psychological problems than those who've been affected by the death of a parent.[6]

Children of divorce are at greater risk of experiencing injury, asthma, headaches, and speech defects than children whose parents remain married.[7]

Children of divorced couples are 50 percent more likely to develop health problems than those in two-parent families.[8]

Children living with both biological parents are 20 to 35 percent more healthy physically than children from broken homes.[9]

Most victims of child molestation come from single-parent households or are the children of drug-ring members.[10]

A child in a female-headed home is ten times more likely to be beaten or murdered.[11]

The Long-Term Effects of Divorce on Children

Six years after a parental marriage breakup, children tend to be "lonely, unhappy, anxious and insecure."[12]

Seventy percent of long-term prison inmates grew up in broken homes.[13]

Problems Relating to Peers

Children of divorce are four times more likely to report problems with peers and friends than children whose parents have kept their marriages intact.[14]

Children of divorce, particularly boys, tend to be more aggressive toward others than children whose parents did not divorce.[15]

Suicide and Divorce

People who come from broken homes are almost twice as likely to attempt suicide than those who do not come from broken homes.[16]

High School Drop-Outs

Children of divorced parents are roughly two times more likely to drop out of high school than their peers who live with both parents still married.[17]

Before you say, "Not *my* kid," remember that the children and teens represented in these statistics are normal kids, probably not much different from yours. Their parents didn't think they would get involved in these things either. Again, we're looking at increased *risks*.

The impact that divorce has on children, in my opinion has been largely underestimated. Obviously, not every child of divorce commits crime or drops out of school. Some do well in school and even become high achievers. However, we now know that even these children experience deep and lasting emotional trauma. For *all* children, their parents' divorce colors their view of the world and relationships for the rest of their lives.

Divorce is no small thing to children. It is the violent ripping apart of their parents, a loss of stability and often a complete shock. While we often think of children as resilient, going through such trauma is a lot to ask of our kids. In light of the fact that most marriages heading for divorce can be salvaged and turned into great marriages, parents should take a long pause before choosing divorce. While it may seem like a good solution, it's not an easy out for you or your kids.

The Impact On You

Editor Jane Bianchi gathered data in an article identifying several surprising consequences of divorce on couples.[18] Here is a summarized list of the key findings:

Anxiety

The future you once pictured no longer exists. Uncertainty can lead to feeling insecure. You might have to move, get a new job, survive on less money than before. Your children may need to change schools or adjust to a back-and-forth arrangement with you and your ex. Anxiety can manifest itself in controlling behavior, such as sending an excessive number of emails to your divorce attorney or emptying your joint bank account to try to take over the finances.

Drastic Weight Change

During or after a divorce, people often turn to "comfort foods" as a temporary "pick-me-up." Others lose their appetite and experience drastic and unhealthy weight loss.

Metabolic Syndrome

Metabolic syndrome occurs when you have several dangerous conditions at once, including high blood pressure, high blood sugar, and high cholesterol. It increases your risk for heart disease, stroke, and diabetes. A study published in *Archives of Internal Medicine* found that women who are divorced (as well as women who are widowed or in unhappy marriages) are more likely to develop metabolic syndrome than women who are in happy marriages.

Depression

After a marriage dissolves, many people feel like failures. The circumstances that contributed to the divorce also play a role. For instance, if your spouse cheated on you, that might destroy your self-confidence. Walfish recommends seeking out a good therapist. Someone who is emotionally removed from the situation can provide valuable support. Therapy can also help you discover why you were drawn to your spouse in the first place—and learn how to avoid this situation altogether.

Cardiovascular Disease

A study published in the *Journal of Marriage and Family* found that middle-aged men and women are at a higher risk of developing cardiovascular disease after going through a divorce, compared with married people of the same age. Middle-aged women who get divorced are more likely to develop cardiovascular disease than middle-aged men who get divorced. The stress of divorce leads to higher levels of inflammation in women, and those levels persist for some time, explains Mark D. Hayward, professor of sociology at the University of Texas at Austin. "Women often take bigger hits in terms of finances, and they tend to stay single longer than men."

Substance Abuse

A 2012 review published in *The Journal of Men's Health* found that divorced men have higher rates of substance abuse, mortality, depression, and lack of social support than married men. "The stress you feel from a divorce is second only to the stress you feel from the death of a spouse," explains study coauthor Dave Robinson, PhD, director of the Marriage and Family Therapy Program at Utah State University. "And men are more likely to ignore the significant impact that divorce has on them."

Insomnia

"In my divorced clients, sleep disruption is very common, as well as nightmares," says Walfish. According to the National Sleep Foundation, insomnia is common among those who are depressed.

Chronic Health Problems

Eating well and exercising regularly are harder if you're feeling depressed or not sleeping well. These unhealthy habits can lead to serious diseases and conditions. A study published in *Journal of Health and Social Behavior* found that divorced or widowed people have 20 percent more chronic health conditions (such as heart disease, diabetes, and cancer) than people who are married.

The intent of this chapter is not to make you feel guilty or judged. It is only to educate you. You may feel that there is no hope for your marriage, that the hurt is too deep to restore the love and relationship you once had. The truth is, your life and marriage can be better and stronger than it was before. In fact, thousands of marriages, situations as complex and painful as yours, have been transformed. I hope these statistics motivate you and provide assurance to keep fighting for your marriage.

what to say

- "For the benefit of our children and our health, I am willing to do whatever it takes to stay together. Would you be willing to reach out for help with our marriage?"
- "Can we agree that divorce should not be considered a serious option for us?"
- "Our commitment to each other can be a huge lesson for our children. Let's show them it's possible to survive difficulties in life."

what to do

- Show your spouse the statistics about divorce in this chapter and do some research on this subject yourself.
- Avoid blaming. Acknowledge how your behavior may have caused your spouse to behave in an undesirable way, perhaps even wanting a divorce.

what to read

- Joshua 10:25
- Job 11:18-19
- Psalm 3:2-6; 147:11

what to pray

Lord, my spouse and I have become one flesh through marriage, and what You have joined together, no man should separate.

Help me let go of my fear of failure. I know Satan would love to separate what You have joined together, and he wants to use my fears to hold me back from living boldly for You. Forgive me for not living in faith, and help me from this moment on to live with bold confidence in You. Lord, help me not compare myself to others. I pray that I can instead keep my eyes on You and live a life that proclaims Your excellence. In Jesus's name I pray, amen.

notes

_____

_____

_____

_____

_____

_____

_____

_____

_____

_____

_____

_____

_____

_____

_____

_____

_____

_____

_____

_____

_____

_____

_____

_____

Week 35

Persevere

I love the words that define perseverance, according to Merriam-Webster: "continued effort to do or achieve something despite difficulties, failure or opposition." Synonyms: persistence, tenacity, determination, staying power, steadfastness, purposefulness.[19]

Each word makes me want to stand on top of a mountain and scream, *"I will never give up!"* As I think about the word perseverance, my mind races through the Bible verses that share the message of this powerful word that each one of us must hold onto as we do this thing called life and marriage.

God knew right from the beginning of time that men and women would need to persevere through this life and walk alongside each other. They would be able to lean on, inspire, hold, love, cry with and encourage one another as they do their "course and ministry of marriage" together to testify to the grace of God. (Yes, our marriages are a ministry to our husband or wife and to the world around us).

My wife, Pam and I have been married for 17 years and only by the grace of God have we been able to come this far. Of course, it's not over, so we will need a whole lot more grace from God and each other to finish well. How have we made it through seventeen years of marriage? Perseverance. We work hard to get through the difficult times by leaning on the Lord.

We try to outdo each other through serving. We try to guard our mouths, minds and hearts so that we reflect love towards one another. And we always, always remember that we cannot allow our feelings to dictate our decisions.

Certainly, what I want for you is to persevere. However, I would be missing the mark if I stopped there. If I told you to stay committed to the relationship no matter how awful your marriage is, that would *fall short of what God intends*. God doesn't command us to be committed to staying married; that is too easy. *He requires us to be committed to loving our spouse.* That is a whole lot harder than just *not filing for divorce*. To love my spouse means I must pursue her, attempt to engage her, actively seek to know her and live my life in ways that are in her best interests. Ouch! How do I do that when I don't feel like it, or she isn't responsive? How do I love when she doesn't give much love in return? What about when I am angry? Or when she has just hurt me? It starts with perseverance—*choosing to stay committed to your goal* (of loving your spouse, of loving God and glorifying Him)—no matter the obstacles you face.

Marriage is tough, but it is one of the most beautiful gifts that one can receive in his or her life. Remember, perseverance is "steadfastness in doing something despite difficulty or delay in achieving success." Continue to finish your course well; run the marriage race showing the unbelieving and believing world that we are not quitters—but doers with persistence, tenacity, determination, and God's power.

what to say

- "I want to persevere through our difficulties, but I don't want us to just coexist. What can I do to make our marriage the best it can be?"
- "I'm trusting God to help us both persevere, in the good times and bad."

what to do

- Depend on God.
- Commit to loving Him and your spouse.
- Remember special moments in your marriage.
- Remind yourself of what you said you were going to do for your spouse and for your marriage. Then take steps to do it.
- Visit refreshyourmarriage.org to get connected with a certified mentor couple who can help you.

what to read

- Romans 12:12
- Galatians 6:9
- Colossians 1:11-12
- 2 Thessalonians 3:13
- James 1:12

what to pray

Dear God, thank You for today. No matter what happens today, help me to endure. Please fill my heart with joy and peace, and enable me to persevere in my marriage. I am thankful for my spouse. Empower us and give us what we need to stand in faith. Remind us of the hope we have in Your Son, Jesus. Help us to lean on You and to trust in Your ways. In Jesus's name, amen!

notes

_____

_____

_____

_____

_____

_____

Week 36

Let God Be Your Guide

To know God's guidance, we must put aside our own will and seek His. The best way to determine God's will in any situation is to empty yourself of your own will, as much as you are able, and to commit yourself to seeking and obeying God's will. Then He will reveal the steps you need to take in the right timing.

If you want to know God's will, you must be willing to do it, even if it contradicts your will. If all you really want is God's approval of your plans, you'll never know His direction. God reveals His will to those who are committed to doing it.

Often we get so caught up doing our own thing that we fail to stop and ask God to reveal His will to us. Or we get into our established routine, and it takes a catastrophe for God to get our attention so He can let us know what He wants us to do.

Stop right now and ask God for His guidance. Then wait and listen to what He might say. "Those who are led by the Spirit of God are the children of God" (Romans 8:14).

Waiting for God isn't easy. We tend to become impatient and take matters into our own hands. When we wait, our faith is tested and our motives undergo purification. "The testing of your faith develops perseverance. Let perseverance finish its work so that you may be mature and complete, not lacking anything" (James 1:3-4). Waiting overcomes the erratic distortions that can be a part of moods and emotions and eventually produces hope (as we see in Romans 5:3-4).

You may hesitate to seek God's guidance because of ongoing and unconfessed sin.

Keep in mind, being tempted isn't sin—surrendering to temptation is sin. Temptation is an opportunity to do what is right by turning from sin. First Corinthians 10:13 (NKJV) states, "No temptation has overtaken you except such as is common to man; but God is faithful, who will not allow you to be tempted beyond what you are able, but with the temptation will also make the way of escape, that you may be able to bear it." The Holy Spirit will prompt us to flee temptation, turn from sin, and seek God.

If you "trust in the Lord with all your heart and lean not on your own understanding" and "in all your ways acknowledge Him," then "He will direct your paths" (Proverbs 3:5-6) for His glory and for your good. Walk daily with Him; be committed to His purpose. He will guide you in all your ways.

Stop trying to figure out the "whys" of life and trust the God who understands you more than you ever could yourself.

what to say (to Jesus):

- "Here I am, Lord. Fully yours. Right now, I feel _____. I am hurting because _____. I am fearful of _____. I am angry about _____. I need you to _____. I trust you because_____."
- "Jesus, here is what happened to me today ..."
- "Jesus, I am tempted to ..."
- "Jesus, I feel Satan tormenting me by ..."
- "Jesus, please help my spouse become ..."

what to do

- Talk out loud to God as if He were sitting next to you. Journal your conversations with Him.
- Confess and surrender your need to control.
- Make a list of all the trials God has carried you through.

what to read

- 1 Samuel 24
- Psalm 46; 62; 117; 121
- Romans 12:2
- 1 Thessalonians 5:16-18

what to pray

Lord, thank You for Your greatness. Thank You that when I am weak, You are strong. Forgive me for trying to fix my situation on my own. Forgive me for running all different directions, spinning my wheels to find help when true help and healing must be found first in You. Forgive me for forgetting how much I need You above everyone and everything else. I ask for Your strength to guide me so that I might not give in to discouragement, deception, and doubt. Help me honor You in all my ways. In Jesus's name, amen.

notes

go on a quest

Week 37

Extend Grace

Grace is the free and unmerited favor of God. Grace is what we need when we have messed up, fallen down, made wrong choices, and sinned. And this is what we receive from God—and what we need to humbly extend to our spouses when they mess up, fall down, make wrong choices, and sin. Your spouse needs to know it's okay to fail, be frustrated, have a hard day, need alone time, or even cry.

Try to see your spouse as God does, through the eyes of mercy. When mercy is lacking, it opens a door to bitter arguments that last for hours. We become self-righteous and demand our spouses address the sins they have committed against us immediately. We feel sorry for ourselves and blame everything on our spouses.

How can you tell if grace is lacking in your marriage? Ask yourself the following questions:

- Do I become frustrated over little things my spouse does?
- Does my spouse have certain behaviors or quirks that irritate me?
- Am I tired of trying to change my spouse?
- Does my spouse accuse me of nagging and nitpicking?

- Do I find myself regularly losing patience and getting snippy with my spouse?
- Do I assume the worst about my spouse or jump to negative conclusions?
- Am I overly critical of my spouse?
- Do I expect my spouse to read my mind, decode my body language, and meet all my needs?

If you answered yes to any of these questions, you might be struggling with extending grace in your marriage. It's possible that grace has been replaced by hurt, frustration, and resentment. These negative feelings toward your spouse could have been slowly building until your heart shut down or hardened. But there's hope.

Your spouse's personality, the home they were raised in, and their current walk with God may make them incapable of ever meeting the needs you have. Only God can meet your every need. Releasing our spouse from these expectations will bless not only them, but you as well.

what to say

- Sometimes it's better to say nothing than to share disappointment and frustrations.

what to do

- Forgive as God forgave you.
- Be slow to anger, exercising patience.
- Put more focus on your spouse's positives than their problems. Believe the best about your spouse.
- Do something unexpected for your spouse. Send a midday text, or bring home a small surprise gift.
- Focus on who your spouse is: a son or daughter of the Most High King, made in God's image.
- Spend time doing something fun together.

what to read

- Romans 3:20-24
- 2 Corinthians 12:8-9
- Ephesians 2:8-9; 4:32
- Hebrews 4:16
- James 4:6
- 2 Peter 1:2

what to pray

Dear Lord, I confess my need for You today. I need Your healing and Your grace in my marriage. I need to be reminded that You work on behalf of those You love. I come to You now and bring You to the places I am hurting. You see where no one else is able to fully understand. You know the pain I've carried. The burdens. The cares. You know where I need to be set free. I ask for Your healing and grace to cover every broken place in my marriage. Every wound. Every heartache. Help me, Lord, to extend the same grace You give me to my spouse and children. Thank You that You will never waste my pain and suffering. I love You and need You. In Jesus's name, amen.

notes

_____

_____

_____

_____

_____

_____

_____

_____

_____

_____

_____

Week 38

Work on Your Weaknesses

Ryan woke up every day plagued by his wife's behavior. She was disrespectful and rude, often became self-righteous, constantly berated him, and regularly reminded him of his faults. No matter what he did, it was never good enough. She was a quick thinker, and Ryan had no chance to win any arguments with her. His heart and mind repeatedly relived every wound until one day, his pastor preached a message titled "The Miracle Starts with You."

The pastor reading Matthew 7:3-5, which tells us to remove the planks in our own eyes before we even consider addressing the speck of dust in someone else's. The sermon reminded Ryan that before we address the sins of those around us, we must first look inward and face our own.

The sermon pierced Ryan's heart and put him on a mission to find and eliminate his own sin patterns. He started to apply the truth to his own heart and slowly, the planks were removed from his eyes. While he fervently worked on his own issues, he extended grace to his wife. She watched him transform into a different man. God healed her through Ryan's actions.

If your husband is unloving, focus on being respectful toward him. If your wife is disrespectful, focus on being loving toward her. Personal growth can be the catalyst for positive change in a relationship. Always look for the areas you can accept responsibility first. When we are willing to be the change we imagine, we have already opened the gate for positive change in our spouse.

Resist the urge to blame your wife for difficulties, even when you know you're doing your best. Blaming always takes you a step backward.

Have you acknowledged your weaknesses? To discover any possible bondages, consider whether any of the following statements are true for you:

- I can't stop a certain behavior that is hurting my marriage.
- I can't stop blaming my partner in my heart and with my mouth.
- I can't stop being negative and thinking about negative things.
- I need alcohol or drugs to get through my day.
- I sometimes don't talk to my spouse for days.
- I keep thinking about the wound my spouse caused.
- I engage in porn and self-gratification multiple times per year.
- I've fallen into sexual sin and can't stop.
- I share personal things with someone I shouldn't.
- I am angry all the time.
- I feel depressed because of my sinful behavior.
- I can't stop having outbursts of anger and cursing.

Even Christians can be in bondage. But you can find freedom. The miracle starts with YOU!

Here are some steps to take toward finding and experiencing freedom:

- Repent to God for your sins and believe in His Son, Jesus, for your salvation.

- Immerse yourself in a Bible-teaching church.
- Apply God's Word to your life.
- Admit you have a problem or addiction.
- Identify any past trauma. (Who has wounded you?)
- Evaluate your reaction to the trauma. (What sinful patterns developed as a result of the trauma?)
- Repent of your sin and break free from the patterns. Rebuke Satan and his followers from your heart, mind, home, and life, in Jesus's name.
- Seek help if you can't find freedom on your own.

Pureheart Ministries (pureheartministries.net) can help you escape sexual bondage and live in freedom. I also recommend Twelve Stone Ministries (twelvestones.org) for counseling.

Whatever is keeping you in bondage, take it seriously and get help to remove it from your life. Your marriage, other relationships, and your life will never be healthy or on solid ground until you do.

God can reach your spouse through your actions and reactions. Remember, give grace to your spouse's sin pattern because "The miracle starts with YOU!

what to say

- "I am guilty of patterns that need to be broken. As I look inward, I see that I'm struggling with _____ and need to find freedom from its influence over me."
- "Is there any area in your life that you feel you are in bondage? How can I specifically be praying for you?"

what to do

- Be honest about the depth of your addiction. Repent and stop the self-destructive behavior.
- Find a resource that is biblical and proven effective to offer freedom.

- Get that resource. It may cost you something, but it may cost you everything if you do not.

what to read

- John 8:36
- Acts 13:38-39
- Romans 8:1-6
- 2 Corinthians 3:17
- Galatians 3:22, 5:1
- Ephesians 6:12
- 1 Peter 2:16

what to pray

Lord, I want to lay everything down before You that weighs heavy on my heart. I desperately need You to transform me into Your likeness. I know that with one touch, one word, You can make me whole. Please forgive me of my sins, cleanse me of my unrighteousness, and begin Your healing from the inside out. Thank You, Lord, for Your unending love for me. Help me start fresh right now to make choices that honor You. In Jesus's name, amen.

notes

_____
_____
_____
_____
_____
_____
_____
_____
_____

Week 39

Avoid the Pitfalls

Marriage takes work and intentionality. Here are the top five traps I see couples fall into when they are lonely, wounded, and want more from their marriage.

Allowing the Small Things to Become Big Things

All couples argue. Happy couples have strategies for dealing with their inevitable disagreements, and they process their feelings so they don't bottle up. They're able to address issues before they become big issues.

Always Having to Be Right

No one is always right. If you try to prove your point, you may win the battle but lose the war. Resist the urge to lecture your spouse or always get in the last word. It's hard to love a know-it-all. Admit when you make a mistake or when you don't have all the answers.

Seeking Friends Who Tell You What You Want to Hear

We often turn to friends or family for comfort when we're hurting. Sometimes all we're really looking for is for them to tell us what we *want* to hear, not what we *need* to hear.

As you seek counsel from friends or family, turn to those who will speak truth to you. People who don't know the Lord will not understand God's teachings on how to endure hardships or how to wait patiently on the Lord. They will not be inclined to forgive and show mercy. They will tell you to run from your pain. This is a time in your life that you really need to rely on people to give you godly advice, not someone who will encourage you to do 'whatever makes you happy.'

Happiness is temporary. True joy comes from knowing Jesus and following His ways. Turn to friends and family who know Jesus and can help you follow Him.

Excessive Social Media

Don't lean on social media when you're lonely. This too can be very problematic. It's easy for unhappy partners to turn to social media for comfort or distraction. Excessive use of social networking and similar sites could indeed not just play a role in compensating for an unhappy relationship but may actually *contribute* to that unhappiness. Take your burdens to someone of the same sex who loves the Lord. Better yet, take your burdens directly to the Lord.

Confiding in the Opposite Sex

If you open yourself up to people of the opposite sex who are in the same boat as you, you may both be tempted to seek solace in each other's arms. Their empathy will feel wonderful. Their words of affirmation will be sweet music to your ears. They'll give you the attention and affection you yearn for. But tiny innocent steps can lead you down a path of terrible destruction.

Leaning on Alcohol, Drugs, or Porn

Alcohol and drugs create a buffer to help people escape their pain and numb their anxiety. Unfortunately, one drink usually leads to another. Your body develops an immunity to your drug of choice, requiring you to up the dosage or find something stronger. Next thing you know, you are in a downward spiral heading towards an addiction which only compounds your problems with greater problems.

Porn is equally dangerous. It has ruined the lives of countless married couples. Real life can never measure up to the hyper-sexualized world of pornography, and exposure to it can rob you of the chance for a natural, fulfilling relationship. This goes for both partners and includes reading erotic fiction.

what to say

- "How can I be more loving or respectful to you?"
- "Thinking about you today made me smile."
- "If we work together to resolve some of our issues, I know we can accomplish anything."
- "Let's remember all the good things God has done for us."
- "Let's imagine all the good things God has planned for us."

what to do

- If there is a small unresolved issue in your marriage that has been weighing heavy on your heart, take it to the Lord and ask for wisdom in addressing it with your spouse before it becomes a big issue.

- Share with your spouse at least one area in which you are proud of them for making a decision that was for the betterment of the marriage/family.

- If you have been turning to alcohol, drugs, or porn, admit it to a godly friend who will hold you accountable to eliminating it from your life.

what to read

- Exodus 23:2
- Psalm 1:1; 107:20; 141:4
- Proverbs 4:14; 9:6; 22:3-14
- Romans 16:17

what to pray

Father God, You are my rock, and I run to You today, believing that You will lift up my heavy arms, that You will fuel me for the tasks You've given me, and that Your joy will completely consume the weakness of my life and make me strong again. I don't want to stay grounded, crippled by limitations and failed attempts. I'm tired of feeble efforts. Lord, I want to mount up with wings like an eagle and not just fly, but soar. Renew my strength, Lord. Fill me with Your supernatural power to overcome each obstacle in my path. With my eyes on You, Lord, with You walking beside me and working through me, I can make it. Thank You, Lord.

notes

_____

_____

_____

_____

_____

_____

_____

_____

_____

_____

_____

_____

_____

_____

_____

_____

_____

_____

_____

_____

Week 40

Become a Humble Warrior

Humility is seeing our place in the world, not as we would have it, but as it really is. The proud have an inflated view of themselves; the humble are content with who they are.

God has a real issue with anyone who is prideful. The Bible tells of countless times when God's wrath was poured out in response to pride.

God fights for the humble. He pours out His grace upon the humble. There is no warrior more powerful than a humble one. There is no leader more effective than a humble one. There is no parent, friend, husband, or wife better than those who are humble. Let humility be the single character trait you strive for the most.

Philippians 2:3 tells us to value others above ourselves and do nothing out of vain conceit. If only we could live that out in our marriages!

I wish I valued Pam above myself all the time, but the truth is, I don't. Selfishness creeps in and Satan whispers in my ear, *What about you, Matt? Don't you deserve more?*

Maybe you've thought, When do I get what I want? or When will it be about me? It's not wrong to have those thoughts. But it's unhealthy to live them out and allow them to direct your path.

Valuing Pam above myself doesn't mean that I never share my opinion or push back on hers. On the contrary, sometimes it's important to stand firm in your conviction. But you can be humble and value your spouse at the same time.

We live in a "me, myself, and I" society today. Everything around us tells us we deserve more, we are entitled to more, and we should indulge ourselves whenever possible. Commercials convince us we are missing out if we don't go, buy, do, and acquire whatever they are peddling. A humble person has the ability to be content with and grateful for what God has given them, including those around them.

Pam has helped me discover the ways I sometimes come across as prideful. I'm on a quest to be humble and it's not easy. I still fail, but it's always on my mind. I want to be humble. I pray for humility.

If you don't choose to become humble, God will humble you. In 1 and 2 Samuel, Saul was given kingship over Israel. He had amazing support from a God-fearing man named Samuel. Unfortunately, Saul turned his back on the wise counsel Samuel offered. God took from him his entire kingdom and gave it to King David.

Marriage requires humility, but if your marriage is suffering it's a struggle to consider your spouse *more important than yourself* (Philippians 2:3). One verse that keeps me more grounded in this area than any other is James 4:6 (ESV): "God opposes the proud, but gives grace to the humble."

When a strong, courageous person wears the cape of humility, there is no limit to their dreams. Strive to be a humble warrior.

"True humility is not thinking less of yourself, it's thinking of yourself less."[20]
—Rick Warren

what to say

- "In what ways can I become more humble?"
- "Please forgive me for elevating myself over you. I value you and want to put your needs before my own."
- "I want to be a humble servant. It will take time, but I am working on it."

what to do

- Ask a trusted friend to share their opinion of the areas where you need to become humble.
- Each day ask God to help you be a "servant" to people.
- This week, deny yourself personal time and serve your spouse with a project that will target their heart. Do a little investigating to find out what would bless them.
- Repent of your pride and ask God for His forgiveness and His blessing.
- In conversations with friends and family, be intentional to ask more questions about them and share less about you.

what to read

- 2 Chronicles 7:14
- Proverbs 11:2; 18:12; 27:2
- Luke 14:11
- Ephesians 4:1-3
- Philippians 4:12
- James 4:10
- 1 Peter 5:5

what to pray

Lord, I come with open hands and an open heart, ready to depend on You to help me through the day and everything it brings. I ask

You for guidance, strength, provision, and protection. Forgive me for my arrogance and pride. Give me a spirit of humility so that I may serve people. Help me become a servant to my spouse and my family, even when it's hard. I will continue to run to You, Lord, for healing, guidance, and encouragement. In Jesus's holy name, amen.

notes

slow and steady

Week 41

Learn from King David

In Psalm 138:6-8 (NLT) David says, "Though the Lord is great, he cares for the humble, but keeps his distance from the proud. Though I am surrounded by troubles, you will protect me from the anger of my enemies. You reach out your hand, and the power of your right hand saves me. The Lord will work out his plans for my life - for your faithful love, O Lord, endures forever. Don't abandon me, for you made me."

It seems like David is saying "Finish what you've started in me. Oh, God, don't quit on me now." King David is one of my favorite people to study in the Bible because I can relate to his passion, his sin, and his remorse.

God chose David to be king of Judah when he was just a boy, but he didn't take the throne for another fifteen years. He was small in stature but had a huge heart and unbridled abilities to worship God. He was a shepherd who played a harp. As he got older he entered into battle with his brothers to fight the Philistines, one of whom was a giant named Goliath, who was nine feet tall and had proven unbeatable.

King Saul, the king of Judah anointed by God, was slowly falling away from God's ways and His favor. Saul was afraid of this giant and unsure What to do. Little David marched into battle with no sword or high-tech weapons, just a sling and a tremendous amount of faith and courage.

With one swing, David slung a rock at the giant and killed him. This act immediately spun him into stardom and fame among God's people. This created jealousy in King Saul. Manipulatively, Saul hired David and gave him unrealistic tasks—which David always accomplished. In his jealousy and rage, Saul attempted to murder David, but to no avail. Multiple times, David had opportunities to kill him easily, but he chose not to.

David told his men, "Who am I to avenge myself? I should not lay one finger on this man who at one time was anointed by God to be king. I will let God avenge me" (1 Samuel 24:12).

Because of David's humility, he trusted God. And God did avenge him.

When David became king, he ruled God's people in amazing ways, bringing more fame to God as he conquered his enemies. God testified about David, calling him "A man after my own heart" (Acts 13:22).

David was not without sin. He committed adultery and murdered one of his own soldiers to cover it up. He suffered the consequences of his sins, but God's affection never left David.

Why was God so affectionate toward David? And what does all this have to do with you and your marriage? Let me focus on four truths from David's story:

- David was patient.
- David was humble and repentant.
- David worshipped God even during times of persecution.
- David feared God more than man.

You can find God's favor, too, by seeking these same attributes.

Be patient. Don't avenge yourself. Let God avenge you in His way and His timing.

Learn how to humbly serve the person who is hurting you. God will honor you.

Worship God during times of turmoil and times of triumph.

David was one of the most beautiful worshipping warriors you will ever read about (2 Samuel 6:14-20). He danced in the streets. His worship was unbridled, like love letters to God.

Can you imagine the President of the United States dancing in the streets with arms lifted up in praise to God, with no fear of politics or the media? No wonder why God loved David so much. Imagine that kind of passionate worship in your life, regardless of your circumstances.

Learn from the victories and failures of King David. God favored him. I want God to favor you, too. He will, if you take the path of David.

what to say

- "I will continue to be patient and wait on the Lord."
- "I want to pursue God's ways (whatever that means), not my own."

what to do

- Take your worship to a whole new level. Pray or sing out loud to God in a way that's out of your comfort level. Do it as unto the Lord and Him only.
- Tell God that you're okay with His timing, even if it takes years to fully sanctify your spouse and rectify your situation. "Your will, not my will, be done."
- Strive to become more like David—a servant, a warrior, and a worshiper—every day.

what to read

- 1 and 2 Samuel

what to pray

Dear Lord, I need Your strength to say 'no' when I'm tempted to surrender to harmful things, or when selfishness takes over and won't let go. I need Your strength to say 'yes' when cowardice and fear nudge me to deny the convictions of my heart. I need Your strength to reach out in love to my spouse. Strengthen me in the power of Your might, O God. Dress me in Your armor so that I can stand firm against the schemes of the devil. I ask all this in the powerful name of Jesus, amen.

notes

_____
_____
_____
_____
_____
_____
_____
_____
_____
_____
_____
_____
_____
_____
_____
_____
_____
_____
_____

Week 42

Learn from Abraham and Sarah

Abraham paved the way for the bloodline of our Lord Jesus Christ. He was not a perfect man, but he was a man of faith.

In his day, having children was almost more important than marriage. God promised Abraham and Sarah they would produce the seed of God's future army of believers. He compared the number of their descendants to the number of stars in the sky.

Before having any children, Abraham and Sarah brought their extended family and belongings from Ur (in the Middle East) to Babylon, then to the land of Canaan, and eventually to Egypt. Along the way, they realized that Sarah was barren.

How could God promise them such a thing, getting their hopes up, if she couldn't have children? What they didn't know at the time was that it wasn't an issue of *whether* they could have children, but *when* they would.

In their ignorance and impatience, they made a series of poor choices, taking the matter into their own hands. Sarah convinced Abraham to have sex with her maidservant. That circumvented God's plan. Their lack of wisdom cost them greatly.

Choosing divorce often becomes our way of thwarting God's plan and taking control ourselves.

Sarah came to despise the maidservant and her son, and she ordered them to be exiled into the desert to die. Once again, Abraham acquiesced to her demands. But God spared the maidservant and her son.

At the age of ninety, God touched Sarah's womb and allowed her to get pregnant. God fulfilled His promise. Through Isaac, a nation was born that leads to the bloodline of Jesus Christ and our salvation.

My parents experienced thirty years of strife, hurt, pain, and loneliness in their marriage before handing over the reins to God. Once they surrendered, they became inseparable. They found unmatched blessings in their love. All the pain and suffering made their joy even better. A deeper love is often birthed out of adversity. That could be the case for you.

Don't circumvent God and take your marriage into your own hands. Trust God for the long haul. He will be with you. Of course, if you (or your children) are in harm's way (physically or emotionally) seek help right away. If you're experiencing an abusive relationship, know that help is available. Contact The National Domestic Violence Hotline, or call 1-800-799-SAFE (7233).

what to say

- "I do not want to put our marriage and family in the hands of lawyers. I want to put my trust in God."
- "God will bring a miracle into our future. I believe it."

what to do

- Each day consciously lay aside your own expectations and surrender to God's plans.
- Replace negative thoughts with positive ones. When you

find yourself having thoughts that bring you down, focus on Scripture that will lift you up.

- In the midst of your trial, ask God to give you patience and help you trust that He knows what's best for you.
- Stay in prayer as your faith is tested.

what to read

- Genesis 13-22 (the story of Abraham and Sarah)
- Hebrews 11:8-12

what to pray

Abba Father, the pressures of life sometimes push me into a corner, rendering me helpless to move forward, not knowing where to turn. Help me not to quit, but rather to keep trusting You. Let me continue to run the race faithfully and to find strength in that safe place, the arms of the Almighty. In Jesus's name, amen.

notes

_____

_____

_____

_____

_____

_____

_____

_____

_____

_____

_____

_____

_____

_____

Week 43

Learn from Joseph

Joseph was one of twelve sons. His father, Jacob, was the son of Abraham's son Isaac. Joseph was the youngest son and was considered Jacob's favorite. His brothers became jealous and feared Joseph would one day be lord over them. So they decided to sell him to an Egyptian slave trader and tell their father he was killed by a wild animal.

As a slave in a foreign land, Joseph was lonely, hurt, confused, betrayed, angry, mistreated, unloved, and disrespected (sound familiar?). Yet he chose to honor God.

While in captivity, God protected him and granted him favor. His master, Potiphar, a captain of the guards, promoted him to lead attendant. While Joseph was tending to his duties, Potiphar's wife tried to seduce Joseph. He ran away from her so fast she tore off his garment. Then she told Potiphar that Joseph attacked her and tried to rape her.

Once again wrongly accused and horribly treated, Joseph got thrown into prison.

Pharaoh, the king, was having nightmares and sent out word to all his people to find someone who could interpret his dreams.

Having heard Joseph interpret the dreams of other prisoners, the prison guards told Pharaoh about Joseph. The king summoned him, and Joseph correctly interpreted the king's dreams.

Pharaoh was so impressed that he promoted Joseph to second-in-command for the entire nation of Egypt.

Joseph became wealthy, powerful, and revered by everyone in the land. He honored God by sharing with the king and all who would listen that his gifts came from God. And God honored him for his faithfulness.

A terrible drought fell on the land, deeply impacting Joseph's father and his brothers. Jacob sent his sons to Egypt to get supplies, grain, and food so they could survive. When they got to Egypt, Joseph recognized them. All the memories rushing back to him must have been overwhelming. He missed his family so much. He hadn't harbored anger, bitterness, or hatred toward them. He had forgiven them and trusted in the Lord to avenge him in God's way, not his.

Joseph's brothers hadn't recognized him yet. When Joseph revealed his identity to them, they were terrified. But Joseph, overcome with emotion, offered his brothers mercy and forgiveness. He blessed them and cared for them and for his father.

Joseph gave his brothers the best land available in Egypt, with permission from the king. They all lived long and prosperous lives under the blessing of their little brother, despite having sold him into slavery.

That's how God works. He showers blessings on us even when we don't deserve it. He is patient with us. He honors those who honor Him. He always comes through in the end. He has a master plan we often can't see. His name will be glorified. His power will be manifested. His truth will be told. The question is, will we trust God and give Him time to unveil His plan?

Joseph never avenged himself, nor did he take matters into his own hands. The Lord gave him favor. God can do that for you, too, even during your despair and loneliness. Give God a chance to unveil His master plan for your life.

what to say

- "I will continue to love you because God is giving me the strength."
- "I respect you and trust God to do a mighty work in our future."

what to do

- Cry out to God. Tell Him how you feel. You don't have to hide your feelings from Him; He can handle them.
- Find a reason to praise God. (There are many).
- Continue to be a servant to your spouse. Serve them this week with something out of the norm:
  - Cook their favorite meal for them.
  - Pray out loud over them.
  - Run errands for them.
  - Offer to watch the children to allow your spouse to do whatever they want.

what to read

- Genesis 37-47 (the story of Joseph)

what to pray

Dear Lord, when all I see is darkness and I feel weak and helpless, help me to feel Your presence, Your love, and Your strength. Help me to live close to You so I can see Your hand, Your purpose, and Your will through all things. I ask this in the powerful name of Jesus, amen.

notes

Week 44

God Blesses Those Who Wait

The purpose of our life on earth is not to be happy or successful, but to grow in the Lord, develop spiritually, and be strengthened through our experiences. How do we do this? The Scriptures give us the answer: We "wait upon the Lord" (Psalm 37:9).

What does that mean? In the Bible, the word *wait* means to hope, to anticipate, to trust. To hope and trust in the Lord requires faith, patience, humility, meekness, long-suffering, keeping His commands, and enduring to the end.

I don't know anyone who likes to wait. Waiting is hard work and at times can test our faith. It's especially difficult when there are no guarantees that our waiting will ever end in this lifetime. A lack of tangible progress on the desires we long for, prayers we've been praying, and news we're waiting to hear can tempt us to become impatient and discouraged, to worry, even to wonder if God cares.

But waiting on the Lord is the key to God's miracles.

Believe me, patience is not my strength. But I know that if I don't wait on the Lord, I'm allowing Satan to take advantage of my impatience. The Enemy organizes the most elaborate campaigns targeted at our impatience. He dangles carrots in front of us in ways we can't even recognize. Doors of amazing opportunity open that we *think* are from the Lord, but are really from Satan.

Maybe that promotion that was offered to you looks attractive because your salary will increase exponentially. Without prayerful consideration and waiting on the Lord to confirm it is part of His plan, it could be the catalyst that destroys your marriage. Longer hours, more travel, time away from family and friends, and increased stress are all ways Satan can deceive and devour.

Maybe you are going to meet with a client who is attractive and separated from their spouse. You are lonely in your marriage, and your feelings explode when you are with them in an "innocent" business meeting. Satan knows your vulnerability and will not hesitate to use this opportunity.

Sally had been spent months begging God to change her husband. She met with a group of women at her church who prayed with her and studied together. But still she saw no change in her husband. One day, Sally decided, "I'm done." When she shared this decision with her friends at church, they tried to encourage her to be patient. "Nope," she replied. "It's over."

She announced to her husband that she was filing for divorce. Shocked, he ran to the Lord, not knowing what else to do. Feeling broken, he committed his life to Christ. God transformed him into a humble, kind, gentle, thoughtful, and patient man. Everyone who knew him before said, "What happened to John?" Even the kids were in awe of their dad's changes.

You might think his actions were all a strategy to change his wife's mind. But one year later, John was more in love with God than ever and still on fire for the Lord. Even when Sally threw daggers at him and shouted, "You're a fake!," he never took it personally.

Sally had begged God to change John, and he became the husband she had been praying for. But Sally didn't care. She ignored God's answer to her prayers and filed for divorce anyway.

John wrote her love letters asking for forgiveness and begging her to give him a chance. She refused. John prayed for her every night. He tried to encourage their children not to turn on her, but they did. They'd seen their dad repent. They also witnessed their mom respond with contempt. That created a confused fury in them that will last a lifetime, outside of a miracle.

John wasn't physically abusive. He wasn't using drugs or alcohol. He wasn't having an affair. He just was a selfish husband without God in his life. Sally didn't give God a chance to show His amazing power and transformation in and through her husband.

Don't let that be you. God wants to restore your marriage, in His timing. Wait on the Lord and He will honor you.

Isaiah 40:30-31 says, "Though youths grow weary and tired, and vigorous young men stumble badly, *yet those who wait on the Lord will gain new strength,* they will mount up with wings like eagles, they will run and not get tired, they will walk and not become weary" (NASB, emphasis added).

what to say

- "Thanks for being you."
- "I'm proud of you for …"
- "I appreciate your God-given gift of …"
- "We are in this together and I will continue to fight for our marriage."

what to do

- Pray to your heavenly Father, as the Savior did, "Thy kingdom come. Thy will be done."
- Resist fretting, refrain from anger, be still, and choose patience.

- See your circumstance as an opportunity to experience God's goodness.
- Make a decision to love your spouse for who they are right now.
- Wait for God's version of the marriage miracle. Look for it to come in a way that is unexpected. The change may not happen in your spouse—It may happen in you.
- Be steadfast.

what to read

- Psalm 27:14; 37:7; 130:5-6
- Isaiah 8:17, 30:15
- Lamentations 3:24-26
- Hosea 12:6
- Micah 7:7

what to pray

Help me, Lord, to be still in Your presence and to wait quietly and patiently before You. Even though the answers to my prayers may be long in coming, I know You are developing within me a patient trust in You and establishing an even firmer faith in Your Word, for Your Word is true and You are a faithful and merciful God. Increase my love and dependence upon You. Make me more like Jesus in every area of my life, so that I may bear much fruit, to your praise and glory. In Jesus's name, amen.

notes

_____
_____
_____
_____
_____

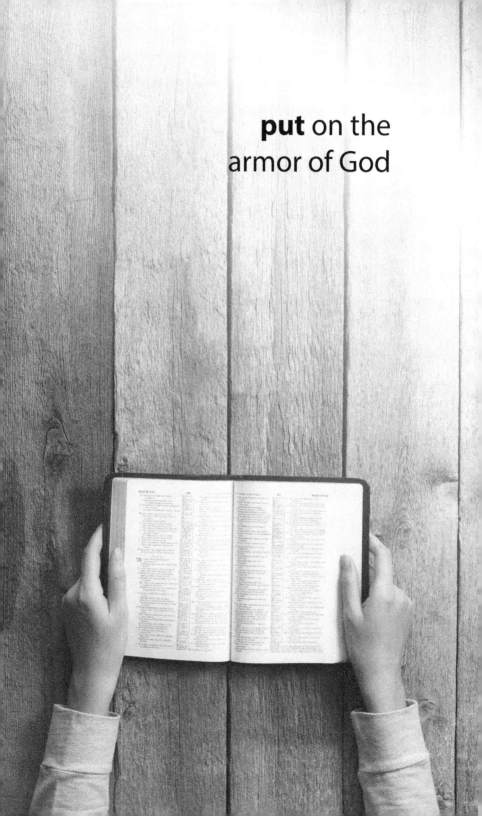

put on the
armor of God

Week 45

The Belt and the Breastplate

This world is a battlefield. Day by day, hour by hour, we face a spiritual warfare and a real Enemy. He wants nothing more than to bring defeat, for his aim is to steal, kill, and destroy. The forces of darkness don't wait for us to be ready for their attack. They're ruthless, determined, and cunning. The devil couldn't care less if we feel prepared or prayed up. In fact, he prefers we're not.

God has given us His Word and Spirit, which are powerful and true, so we'll have the wisdom and protection to stand against the Enemy.

In Ephesians 6, Paul tells a large group of children, parents, servants, and their masters to put on the armor of God.

> Be strong in the Lord and in his mighty power. Put on the full armor of God, so that you can take your stand against the devil's schemes. For our struggle is not against flesh and blood, but against the rulers, against the authorities, against the powers of this dark world and against the spiritual forces of evil in the heavenly realms. Therefore, put on the full armor of God, so that when the day of evil comes,

you may be able to stand your ground, and after you have done everything, to stand. Stand firm then, with the belt of truth buckled around your waist, with the breastplate of righteousness in place, and with your feet fitted with the readiness that comes from the gospel of peace. In addition to all this, take up the shield of faith, with which you can extinguish all the flaming arrows of the evil one. Take the helmet of salvation and the sword of the Spirit, which is the word of God. And pray in the Spirit on all occasions with all kinds of prayers and requests. With this in mind, be alert and always keep on praying for all the Lord's people. Pray also for me, that whenever I speak, words may be given me so that I will fearlessly make known the mystery of the gospel, for which I am an ambassador in chains. Pray that I may declare it fearlessly, as I should (Ephesians 6:10-20).

Why should we put on the full armor of God? So we can withstand the devil's schemes. Wrapping yourself in the armor of God is a long-term plan to stay strong and resist the devil's countless attacks.

Paul starts with the belt of truth. This is the foundation. In our walk with Christ, we may struggle with deceit, lies, and denial. No battle can be won if truth is not the foundation. That is why you need to be honest about yourself. From the depths of truth, you shall stand.

"The truth will set you free but first it will make you miserable."[21]

—James A. Garfield

Truth can't set you free unless you pursue it and allow it to permeate your life. Have you been honest about the depths of your sinful patterns and habits? Have you taken them to the cross? Have you found a desperation for God and His mercy? Have you found truth in who Jesus is? If so, great! You have put on the first piece of armor.

Step two is putting on the breastplate of righteousness. Proverbs 24:16 tells us a righteous man falls seven times and keeps getting up. The key to righteousness isn't spiritual perfection. It's falling, getting up, then falling and getting up again. Keep pursuing God. Repent of your sin and keep being sanctified by Jesus. When you fall, humbly share your failure with godly people.

Righteousness is given to us through our faith in Christ. It cannot be earned, manufactured, or measured. Paul says in Romans 3 that believers inherit the clothing of righteousness through Jesus's sacrifice on the cross. Because of His death and your faith, you became righteous. When you fall, get up and run forward with confidence.

what to say (to yourself)

- "I am righteous."
- "I am honest."
- "I am saved."
- "I am truthful."
- "I cannot be separated from God's love."
- "I am a saint. Though I may struggle with sin, I am not mastered by it."

what to do

- Continue to pursue the truth of the gospel.
- Seek counseling if you are struggling with areas of bondage.
- Live boldly in the confidence that you are holy and righteous because of your faith in Jesus.

- Give your spouse the same confidence you have if they believe in Jesus Christ.

what to read

- Psalm 34:17
- Proverbs 24:16
- Romans 3
- 1 John 4:4

what to pray

Dear Lord, I know I am a sinner and fall short of Your glory, but I ask You for mercy. Please continue to wrap me in Your righteousness. Enable me to continue to get up and run after You when I fail. I pray that Your truth will guide me like a bright star in the night. I pray that I may be open to hear truth and allow it to sanctify me. In Jesus's name, amen.

notes

_____
_____
_____
_____
_____
_____
_____
_____
_____
_____
_____
_____
_____
_____
_____

Week 46

The Shoes and the Shield

The next piece of armor Paul tells us about are shoes.… "and with your feet fitted with the readiness that comes from the gospel of peace" (Ephesians 6:15).

What does it mean to have your feet "fitted with the readiness that comes from the gospel of peace"? Understand the gospel well enough for your feet to take you to places that need to hear it. Be ready to share the gospel with your children, your friends, or a stranger. If God has given you the knowledge of the good news, why wouldn't you be eager to share it with others?

As soldiers of Christ, we must put on "gospel shoes" that allow us to march wherever the Lord leads. Satan will try to place obstacles in our path, but in Jesus's strength we can move forward, following the Lord, obeying Him, and advancing the gospel.

Paul's next piece of armor is the shield of faith. "In addition to all this, take up the shield of faith, with which you can extinguish all the flaming arrows of the evil one" (Ephesians 6:16).

I enjoy playing the game of bid euchre with my family, especially my mother-in-law. I often make high-risk bids. I was once asked, "Why do you make such risky bids?" I answered jokingly, "Faith and courage, baby!" That slogan has stuck for years with my family. We all get a good laugh out of it, whether I win big or lose big.

All joking aside, this reflects how I live my life. Big faith is necessary for big dreams, which can lead to big miracles and big blessings.

Jesus tells us that if we would have faith as small as a mustard seed, we could move mountains (Matthew 17:20). This kind of faith doesn't come from within us. It is God's gift. He gives each of us a measure of faith (Romans 12:3). As we walk with Him, that faith grows until it becomes a shield, protecting us and allowing us to live a victorious life in Christ.

Your armor of God will rise and fall based on your faith and courage. Do you have faith in His power and ability to help you endure? Do you have faith that He has defeated your enemies? Do you have faith that He can turn your hopeless situation around? Do you have faith that even if you are abandoned by your spouse or your spouse doesn't change, you can endure?

Paul the apostle tells us to "walk by faith, not by sight" (2 Corinthians 5:7). The world would tell you that's crazy. It would analyze the symptoms and behavior in your spouse and tell you to divorce them because you deserve better. It would tell you to open your eyes.

Paul tells us the opposite. Don't walk by sight but by faith in Jesus. Walk that path with courage and confidence, even if people scoff at you.

Noah had faith that led to the human civilization being saved. Moses had faith that led millions out of captivity and into the Promised Land. Elijah had faith that called down fire from God. David had faith and God helped him conquer all the land. The apostles had faith to cast out demons, heal the sick, and start the church as we know it today.

When Satan attacks with doubts, the shield of faith turns aside the blow. When temptations come, faith keeps us steadfast in following

Jesus. With faith we are able to withstand all the devil's fiery darts.

What miracles lie out there anxiously waiting for your faith to be unleashed?

what to say

- "I have faith in God's ability to transform our marriage."
- "I have faith that God can make me into the person He wants me to be."
- "I have faith that God's Word is true and is my guide."

what to do

- Continue to serve your spouse in spite of their behavior.
- Allow God's Word to direct your steps.
- Let your feet take you to a place to serve this week. Pick something that stirs your heart.

what to read

- Proverbs 30:5
- Isaiah 40:28-31
- Romans 10:15
- Hebrews 11:1
- 2 Thessalonians 3:3

what to pray

Lord, I ask for forgiveness in my lackadaisical approach to the gospel and my lack of faith. I will continue my quest to know enough about the gospel to make a difference in the life of others. I will let my feet take me to the lost, the broken, and the hopeless. I will allow my faith in You to shine and grow. I have faith that You will reveal Yourself to me more and more. I have faith that You love me and are sanctifying me. I have faith that You will provide my every need. I have faith that You will go before me and pave a way that lines up with Your perfect plan and purpose for my life. I have faith that You will never leave me or forsake me. In Jesus's name, amen.

notes

_____

_____

_____

_____

_____

_____

_____

_____

_____

_____

_____

_____

_____

_____

_____

_____

_____

_____

_____

_____

_____

_____

_____

_____

Week 47

The Helmet

Paul's next piece of armor is the helmet of salvation. "Take the helmet of salvation and the sword of the Spirit, which is the word of God. And pray in the Spirit on all occasions with all kinds of prayers and requests" (Ephesians 6:17-18).

Soldiers use helmets to protect the most vital part of their body, their heads. A head wound would interfere with a person's ability to use their mind to think. Like a helmet covering our heads, our salvation protects our minds from being dealt a deathblow. Those who are in Christ cannot ultimately be defeated by Satan's schemes.

With the helmet of salvation securely in place, we can receive tremendous hope and comfort by focusing on the incredible sacrifice Jesus Christ made to save us. This hope protects our minds from the discouragement, despair, and lies of this world that the Enemy uses as distractions.

When we have a sure knowledge of our salvation, we will not be moved by Satan's deceptions. When we are certain that we are in Christ, with our sins forgiven, we will have a peace that nothing can disturb. The most important thing for you to have at all times is an assurance of your salvation.

Can we be certain of our salvation? Yes! "If we confess our sins, He [Jesus] is faithful and just to forgive us our sins and purify us from all unrighteousness" (1 John 1:9). "And this is testimony: God has given us eternal life, and this life is in His Son. Whoever has the Son has life" (1 John 5:11-12a).

This assurance of salvation offers us the deepest security for our lives here on earth. Nothing is better for your mind than standing on the assurance of your salvation in Jesus Christ. It is secure and it lasts forever. Our "helmet of salvation" gives us confidence knowing we will emerge victorious, because Christ has already won the victory.

what to say (to secure your salvation)

Dear Lord, I know that I am a sinner and that I cannot save myself. By faith I want to receive Your gift of salvation. I am ready to trust You as my Lord and Savior. Thank You, Jesus, for coming to earth. I believe You are the Son of God who died on the cross for my sins and rose from the dead on the third day. Thank You for bearing my sins and giving me the gift of eternal life. Come into my heart, Lord Jesus, and be my Savior. Amen.

what to do

- If you have prayed this prayer in sincere faith, put your initials by the prayer along with today's date as a reminder that you have come to Christ in faith, trusting Him as your Lord and Savior.
- Share with someone your decision to follow Christ.

what to read

- Matthew 10:28
- John 10:27-29
- Romans 10:9, 12:1-2

- 1 Corinthians 1:18
- 2 Corinthians 10:5
- Hebrews 11:6

what to pray

Glorious Father, I thank You for Your unconditional love. Thank You for showing me how great Your love is by sending Your Son to die for me. Thank You for the precious gift of eternal life through Christ Jesus, my Lord. Your majestic name fills the earth! Your glory is higher than the heavens! I will praise Your name forever, for You have all wisdom and power. I put my hope in You, Lord. You are my help and my shield. In the powerful name of Jesus, amen.

notes

_____

_____

_____

_____

_____

_____

_____

_____

_____

_____

_____

_____

_____

_____

_____

_____

_____

_____

Week 48

The Sword

"Take the helmet of salvation and the *sword of the Spirit,* which is the word of God. And pray in the Spirit on all occasions with all kinds of prayers and requests" (Ephesians 6:17-18, emphasis added).

Just as every Roman soldier was equipped with a sword, every believer is equipped with the Word of God. A sword can be used for both offense and defense. The sword of the Spirit is the only weapon of offense listed in the armor of God.

God's Word, the Bible, is described as "alive and active, sharper than any double-edged sword" (Hebrews 4:12a). Jesus used this weapon when Satan tempted Him in the wilderness. To each of Satan's efforts to lead Him into sin, Jesus replied, "It is written ..." and proceeded to quote Scripture to destroy Satan's temptations.

God's Word is truth (John 17:17). That's why it's so powerful. It is important that we study the Bible and become familiar with its truths.

We can't effectively defend Scripture if we are not intimately familiar with everything it teaches. We must read our Bible and study it, then conform our lives to its truth.

If we memorize Scripture, it will be readily available when attacks come. If we meditate on it day and night, it will be our ultimate weapon against Satan.

Do you sometimes feel weak? Do you find yourself giving in to temptation when you really want to overcome? Are you discouraged? We all face these moments. But clothed in the full armor God, the weakest of His children will be strong in the Lord and in the power of His might.

You may wonder, "How do I put on the full armor of God?" It isn't as difficult as you might think. All the pieces of the armor are found in a relationship with Jesus. Paul said, "clothe yourself with the Lord Jesus Christ" (Romans 13:14). When you give yourself to Jesus and "put on" His righteousness, you are clothed in the whole armor of God.

After Paul's description of the armor, he closes by reminding us in verse 18 to "pray in the Spirit on all occasions." Ask God for help clothing yourself in His armor daily, so you can stay alert and stand strong against the devil's schemes.

what to say

- "Would you be interested in us doing a Bible study or devotional together?"
- "I would like to get in the habit of praying with you daily. What are your thoughts?"

what to do

- Commit to reading your Bible daily. Select a time that is realistic and carve out the same time every day to spend with the Lord. Make it a habit.
- Join a Bible study in your church or community.
- Memorize Scripture. Start with one verse a week.
- Journal your prayers.

what to read

- Psalm 119:97-98, 119:105
- Matthew 7:24-25
- Luke 11:28
- John 1:1
- 2 Timothy 3:16-17
- Hebrews 4:12
- James 1:22
- 1 Peter 2:2

what to pray

Thank You, Lord, for Your Word. Your Word is the truth, the life, and the light. It is nourishment for my soul and refreshment to my spirit. Lord, I desire to study Your Word through the guidance of Your Holy Spirit so that I may grow in grace, in spiritual maturity, and in the faith I confess. As I study Your Word, may Your name be exalted and lifted up, for You alone are worthy of praise and worship; You alone are holy and good. Open my eyes to see Your truth. Open my ears to hear Your voice. Open my heart to receive what You have for me. And open my lips to speak only that which glorifies Your name. In the name of Jesus Christ I pray, amen.

notes

_____
_____
_____
_____
_____
_____
_____
_____
_____

define victory
then seize it

Week 49

What Does Victory Look Like?

"Defeat in doing right is nevertheless victory."[22]

—Frederick W. Robertson

Victory is defined in many ways. What does victory look like to you? Often people think of victory in their marriage this way:

- My spouse changes their behavior, and we live in peace.
- My spouse forgives me, and we reconcile.
- My spouse gets saved, and we become happy.
- My spouse and I fall in love again.
- Our marriage thrives and life is good.
- Our intimacy is restored and I feel secure.
- My spouse meets my needs and I am satisfied.
- My spouse takes responsibility for their behavior and we move forward.
- My spouse attends church and we go together as a family.
- My spouse finds freedom from bondage, addiction, and sin and I forgive them.

- My spouse is respectful and I feel respected.
- My spouse is loving and I feel loved.

These are great descriptors that represent victory in marriage. However, if you define victory based solely on the results, and the results fall short of your expectations, you will feel defeated and in despair, with no hope of ever finding victory. When you place all your stock in your spouse doing (or not doing) something in order for you to find victory, Satan wins. You give him the upper hand in deceiving you to believe your spouse is your savior.

Victory will be found when you respond by letting go of life your way; when you put aside your will and sell out completely to the will of God.

Even if you followed this quest to the letter and completely immersed yourself in the arms of Jesus, but your spouse never changed, that is still victory! Submitting your life fully to the grace of God and rising up to the fullness of the Holy Spirit is victory! Falling in love with Jesus is victory! Obeying His Word is victory! Fearing God is victory! Becoming free of anger, bitterness, hate, bondage, worry, and blame is victory! Loving someone who is unlovable is victory! Respecting someone who is hard to respect is victory!

God wants you to find victory over darkness. It won't come easy. But He will give you supernatural strength to endure and the ability to find true joy that comes only from Him.

what to say

- "Our strife has driven me to my knees and into the arms of God, where victory is found. For that I am grateful."

what to do

- Remind yourself that your identity is in Christ above all else.

- Separate yourself from your spouse's roller-coaster ride with God and allow your steadfastness to be the measure of victory.

- Sit down with your children this week and share with them how they can find victory in their lives. Help them understand what victory looks like when they place their trust in Jesus.

what to read

- Deuteronomy 20:4
- Proverbs 21:31
- 1 Corinthians 10:13; 15:57
- Ephesians 6:13
- 1 John 5:3-5

what to pray

Heavenly Father, thank You for the kind of victory that turns problems into testimonies. I pray that in Christ I may be steadfast in everything, knowing that it is in You alone that my victory over the world, my flesh, and the devil is secure. Lord, I ask that You turn all my defeats into complete victory and that Your glory be seen in my life. I ask this in the name of Jesus, amen.

notes

Week 50

What If Your Spouse Doesn't Change?

"Divorce is the one human tragedy that reduces everything to cash."[23]

—Rita May Brown

What can you do if your spouse doesn't change? You've exercised endurance, gained personal victories, and waited on the Lord for a miracle. Now what?

Can you divorce your spouse? Yes. You have free will. Should you divorce your spouse? Christians who are experiencing marriage trouble often wonder, "Is it okay with God that I divorce my spouse?"

What does the Bible say about divorce? Let's look at what God's Word says about three areas: selecting the right partner, divorce, and remarriage. In the sections below I will be paraphrasing Scripture, so be sure you read and study the Bible for yourself.

Selecting the Right Partner

Second Corinthians 6:14-17 says, don't marry someone who isn't a Christian, and don't get in partnership with anyone who isn't a believer. If you do, there may be trouble.

In Deuteronomy 7:3, King Solomon was told not to marry a foreign woman who worshiped false gods. He did it anyway and brought great harm to his children.

Divorce

In Matthew 5:31-32, Jesus told His followers not to divorce unless there was an issue with adultery.

In Matthew 19:3-8, Jesus told the Pharisees not to divorce, without giving any allowances for adultery. He said, "What God has joined together let no man separate." He explained that divorce was permitted in Moses's time due to the hardness of their hearts.

Mark 10:2-12 records Jesus saying the same thing as in Matthew 19:3-8.

In Luke 16:18, Jesus said if someone divorces their spouse and marries another, they are committing adultery, and anyone who marries someone who was married before is also committing adultery.

In 1 Corinthians 7:39, Paul taught that a married person is bound to their spouse as long as they live unless the spouse dies; then they are permitted to remarry. But the person they remarry must belong to the Lord.

In Romans 7:2-3, Paul taught that if a married person has sexual relations with anyone other than their spouse during their lifetime, they are committing adultery.

Deuteronomy 22 provides detailed laws given during the time of Moses for sexual violations. It shows the level of seriousness in which God views marriage.

Malachi 2:16 (NASB) says that God hates divorce.

In 1 Corinthians 7:10-11, Paul says a woman should not leave her husband, but if she does, she is to remain single or reconcile to him. In verses 12-16 he states that if a believer marries an unbeliever, or if someone becomes a believer and their spouse doesn't, the believer should not divorce the unbeliever. They should stay together in hopes that the unbeliever will become sanctified through the salvation of the believer (in other words, they would find Christ because of the believing spouse). But if the unbelieving spouse leaves, the believer is not bound.

Remarriage

Luke 16:18 says that if a man divorces his wife and marries another woman, he commits adultery. And the man who marries a divorced woman commits adultery.

First Corinthians 7:15 states believers are not bound to marriage if an unbelieving spouse abandons them.

According to these passages, there are only two scenarios in which a believer is released from their marriage vows, in God's eyes: (1) If the spouse commits the sexual sin of adultery; (2) If the unbelieving spouse abandons the believer.

I don't believe the abandonment mentioned in 1 Corinthians 7:15 is referring to a one-time occurrence of sexual sin as a biblical right to divorce. That would not line up with Jesus's pattern of challenging us to forgive seventy times seven (Matthew 18:21-22 NASB) and the story of Hosea, who married a prostitute and stayed loyal to her for the rest of his life as God had instructed (Hosea 1-4).

It also doesn't line up with the pattern of God's analogies of His marriage to us. He often refers to our relationship with Him as a marriage, and then says, "My people have prostituted against me over and over, yet I still love them" (Hosea 2). His people worship false gods, but when they returned to Him, He always took them back (Jeremiah 3:1-4). If it's God's pattern to be merciful, how can we refuse to be merciful to others and not forgive their sins?

If your spouse is continually cheating, with no repentance and no indication they are ever going to stop, I'd call that abandonment and support the right to divorce. But we must take into account the times when Jesus gave no provision for divorce and stated they should remain married.

When Jesus gave the one condition by which He allowed divorce in Matthew 5:31-32, the original word translated "adultery" was the Greek word *porneia*, which means "fornication." And with this one condition, He said nothing about remarriage.

The Bottom Line

I hope these biblical passages about marriage and divorce give you a strong conviction to fight for your marriage. Or, if you have studied the Bible and prayed for God to direct you and believe your situation qualifies for the narrow circumstances that biblically justify divorce, that you will do so with a high level of caution and assurance.

Even if you have biblical grounds to divorce, you don't have to exercise it. After all, divorce will deeply impact you, your children, your extended family, and your finances, whether it's justified or not. If you show your spouse mercy, God may bless you abundantly. I urge you to move forward with whatever you truly believe God wants for you.

what to say (to your unfaithful spouse)

- "Even if you never change, I am committed to this marriage."
- "After studying Scripture, I realize how passionate God is about marriage. In obedience to God, I am committed to working on our relationship, starting with myself."

what to do

- If you're considering divorce, seek counsel from the pastor or elders at your church to help you determine if you have a biblical right to do so. But don't stop there. Prayerfully seek God's wisdom. He is your best Counselor.

- If your spouse is faithful and wants to remain in the marriage, continue to unconditionally love and respect them. Find your satisfaction in the Lord and fellowship with other believers.

- Visit refreshyourmarriage.org to get connected with a certified mentor couple who can help you.

what to read

Carefully read all the Scriptures mentioned in this week's devotion.

what to pray

Lord, change me. Whether my spouse changes or not, I need You to align my heart with Yours. Help me to stay focused on changing my behavior. I relinquish control over my spouse to You and ask that You transform them in ways that only You can. Help me to see my spouse through Your eyes. Allow me to see what is in their heart rather than the pain that is in mine. My pain can distort my perceptions and create greater barriers between us. Give me Your love for my spouse. In the precious name of Your Son, Jesus, amen.

notes

_____

_____

_____

_____

_____

_____

_____

_____

_____

Week 51

Understand God's Definition

> Jesus replied: "'Love the Lord your God with all your heart
> and with all your soul and with all your mind.' This is the first
> and greatest commandment. And the second is like it: 'Love
> your neighbor as yourself.' All the Law and the Prophets hang
> on these two commandments."
>
> (Matthew 22:37-40)

We are to love our Creator with all of our heart, soul, and mind and love our neighbor as ourselves. That is God's definition of victory.

Are you able to stand by faith even when everything is falling apart? Or do you look at what is happening in your life and conclude that God must be punishing you or that you must be out of His will? If you are living in fear and confusion, you can overcome the Enemy by faith. If you get to the place where you can stand by faith despite unchanging, even disastrous circumstances, you have victory!

There will be times when everything seems to indicate that God is not with you. You won't be able, no matter how hard you try, to reconcile your circumstances to God's faithfulness. You may feel mad, afraid, betrayed by God. You will think that God must have forsaken you, or this could not have happened.

Don't allow your circumstances to rule your faith. Trust God, not your own understanding.

You may feel like you're jumping off a cliff and expecting God to catch you. But on the basis of Christ's victory for you, He has promised to work on your behalf if you open yourself to Him.

what to say (to God)

- "I will run hard after You. I will run the race. I will stay strong and believe."
- "I claim victory in You despite my circumstances."
- "I love You. I will try with all my might to not allow my faith to be determined by my circumstances. I know You are near and will never forsake me."

what to do

- Write down ten things God has blessed you with over the last six months.
- Ask your friends to share with you any positive changes they have seen in you over the last six months.

what to read

- Deuteronomy 1:30-31; 31:8
- Isaiah 45:2

what to pray

Lord, You are the good Shepherd. You know Your sheep and Your sheep know You. I trust You to put a new spirit in me and my spouse. I ask that You remove from our hearts any bitterness or resentment and give us hearts of love and peace. Help us to not conform any longer to the pattern of this world but to be transformed by the renewing of our minds. In Jesus' name, amen.

notes

Week 52

Seize Victory

"You did not choose me, but I chose you and appointed you
so that you might go and bear fruit—fruit that will last—and
so that whatever you ask in my name the Father will give you."

(John 15:16)

Congratulations! You are in the final week of this quest. Although
our involvement is ending, your adventure is just beginning. The
miracle started with you and will continue with you as you find
your calling and purpose in life.

It will provide great direction to discover the unique spiritual
gift that God has given you. The Holy Spirit distributes these
gifts freely; they cannot be earned or purchased. God gives them
according to His good pleasure.

A spiritual gift is not a natural talent, a fruit of the Spirit, or a
response to a situation. Spiritual gifts are distinct demonstrations
of the Holy Spirit, given by God and empowered by the Holy
Spirit in a believer's life. Each of us should use whatever gifts we
are given to serve others, faithfully administering God's grace in its
various forms.

What spiritual gifts has God given you?

- Evangelism?
- Prophecy?
- Teaching?
- Exhortation?
- Shepherding?
- Serving?
- Mercy-Showing?
- Giving?
- Administration?

God wants to work through you to bless others. You are just as important to God as any major prophet in the Bible. God wants to use you as much as He used the apostle Paul or any of the disciples.

Not everyone has the same calling, but we are all called. It's time to explore and exercise your spiritual gifting as you proceed to the next exciting part of your spiritual journey.

what to say (to God)

- "Here I am, God. Now what?"
- "Lord, please reveal to me Your calling and purpose for my life. I choose Your way, not mine. I want to follow the plans and purposes You have set before me."
- "Lord, I am grateful for You. Please let Your anointing fall upon me."

what to do

- Find a spiritual gift assessment to help you discover your gift.
- Write down five things that "light your fire." Pursue one with tiny steps and see if God's fruit goes before you. Let the fruit confirm your direction and your calling.

what to read

- Psalm 16:11
- Proverbs 16:9
- Jeremiah 29:11
- Romans 8:28
- Ephesians 2:10; 3:20
- Philippians 2:13

what to pray

Lord, I ask You to give me and my spouse the spirit of wisdom and revelation so that we may know You better. I pray that the eyes of our hearts will be enlightened in order to carry out Your will for our lives. Lord, I know You are able to do immeasurably more than we ask or can even imagine, according to Your power that is at work within us. Lord, remove our sinful natures and fill us with the fruit of the Spirit, which is love, joy, peace, patience, kindness, goodness, faithfulness, gentleness, and self-control. In Jesus's name, amen.

notes

_____

_____

_____

_____

_____

_____

_____

_____

_____

_____

_____

_____

We are extremely proud of you for completing this quest. You are a true warrior. Feel free to share with us your journey and how God is being glorified through you. May God bless you for your faithfulness.

Matt & Pam Loehr

Founders of Dare to be Different
matt@daretobedifferent.com
pam@daretobedifferent.com

References

1. Simon, Harvey B. "Giving thanks can make you happier." *Healthbeat,* Harvard Health Publishing, health.harvard.edu/healthbeat/giving-thanks-can-make-you-happier. 29 February 2020.

2. Dove, Laurie L. "How do you criticize something without being a jerk?" 27 September 2013. How Stuff Works.com. science.howstuffworks.com/life/inside-the-mind/emotions/criticize-without-jerk.htm. 20 December 2019.

3. Zenger, Jack and Folkman, Joseph. "The Ideal Praise-to-Criticism Ratio." 15 March 2013. Harvard Business Review, hbr.org/2013/03/the-ideal-praise-to-criticism. 20 December 2019.

4. Cherlin, Andrew J. *Marriage, Divorce, Remarriage.* Harvard University Press, 1981.

5. Hill, Peter. "Recent Advances in Selected Aspects of Adolescent Development." *Journal of Child Psychology and Psychiatry,* vol. 34, no. 1, 1993, pp. 69-99.

6. Emery, Robert E. *Marriage, Divorce and Children's Adjustment.* Sage Publications, 1988.

7. Dawson, Deborah A. "Family Structure and Children's Health and Well-Being: Data from the 1988 National Health Interview Survey on Child Health." *Journal of Marriage and the Family,* vol. 53, no. 3, August 1991, pp. 573-584.

8. Angel, Ronald and Worobey, Jacqueline L. "Single Motherhood and Children's Health." *Journal of Health and Social Behavior,* March 1988.

9. Dawson, Deborah A. "Family Structure and Children's Health and Well-Being: Data from the 1988 National Health Interview

Survey on Child Health." *Journal of Marriage and the Family*, vol. 53, no. 3, August 1991, pp. 573-584.

10. Amneus, Daniel. *The Garbage Generation*. Primrose Press, 1990.

11. Amneus, Daniel. *The Garbage Generation*. Primrose Press, 1990.

12. Wallerstein, Judith S. "The Long-Term Effects of Divorce on Children." *Journal of the American Academy of Child and Adolescent Psychiatry*, vol. 30, no. 3, May 1991, pp. 349-360.

13. Horn, Wade and Bush, Andrew. Fathers, *Marriage and Welfare Reform*. Hudson Institute, 1997.

14. Breen, Dorothy T. and Crosbie-Burnett, Margaret. "Moral Dilemmas of Early Adolescents of Divorced and Intact Families: A Qualitative and Quantitative Analysis." *Journal of Early Adolescence*, May 1993.

15. Emery, Robert E. *Marriage, Divorce and Children's Adjustment*. Sage Publications, 1988.

16. Velez, Carmen N. and Cohen, Patricia. "Suicidal Behavior and Ideation in a Community Sample of Children: Maternal and Youth Reports." *Journal of the American Academy of Child and Adolescent Psychiatry*, vol. 27, no. 3, May 1988, pp. 349-356.

17. McLanahan, Sara and Sandefur, Gary. *Growing Up with a Single Parent: What Hurts, What Helps*. Harvard University Press, 1997.

18. Bianchi, Jane. "8 Surprising Ways Divorce Affects Your Health." 8 February, 2015. 2020 Hearst Magazine Media, Inc. prevention.com/sex/relationships/a20448176/divorce-and-health-effects/. 29 February 2020.

19. "Perseverance." Merriam-Webster.com Dictionary, Merriam-Webster, .merriam-webster.com/dictionary/perseverance. 9 Mar. 2020.

20. "Rick Warren Quotes." BrainyQuote.com. BrainyMedia Inc, 2020. 24 January 2020. brainyquote.com/quotes/rick_warren_395865.

21. "James A. Garfield Quotes." BrainyQuote.com. BrainyMedia

Inc, 2020. 24 January 2020. brainyquote.com/quotes/james_a_garfield_140609.

22. "Frederick W. Robertson Quotes." Christian-quotes.ochristian.com. oChristian.com, 2019. 24 January 2020. christian-quotes.ochristian.com/Frederick-W.-Robertson-Quotes/page-2.shtml.

23. "Rita Mae Brown Quotes." BrainyQuote.com. BrainyMedia Inc, 2020. 24 January 2020. brainyquote.com/quotes/rita_mae_brown_383402.

Images

Cover: Rawpixel.com/shutterstock.com

Page ix: Yauheniya Katliar/shutterstock.com

Page 1: Yelliiz/shutterstock.com

Page 23: sezer66/shutterstock.com

Page 41: wavebreakmedia/shutterstock.com

Page 59: GRJ Photo/shutterstock.com

Page 81: fotohunter/shutterstock.com

Page 99: Mariia Khamidulina/shutterstock.com

Page 117: Robert_s/shutterstock.com

Page 135: Syda Productions/shutterstock.com

Page 153: AstroStar/shutterstock.com

Page 175: Sanchik/shutterstock.com

Page 193: Seekmedia/shutterstock.com

Page 211: 4Max/shutterstock.com

Page 229: Deer Worawut/shutterstock.com